Contents

Reflect and review 77

NEBS
MANAGEMENT
DEVELOPMENT

SUPER SERIES

THIRD EDITION
Managing People

Motivating
People

Published for

&‌ NEBS Management   *by*

Pergamon
Flexible
Learning

Pergamon Flexible Learning
An imprint of Butterworth-Heinemann
Linacre House, Jordan Hill, Oxford OX2 8DP
225 Wildwood Avenue, Woburn, MA 01801-2041
A division of Reed Educational and Professional Publishing Ltd

ℛ A member of the Reed Elsevier plc group

OXFORD   AUCKLAND   BOSTON
JOHANNESBURG   MELBOURNE   NEW DELHI

First published 1986
Second edition 1991
Third edition 1997
Reprinted 1998, 1999, 2000

British Library Cataloguing in Publication Data
A catalogue record for this book is available from the British Library

ISBN 0 7506 3314 X

Whilst every effort has been made to contact copyright
holders, the author would like to hear from anyone
whose copyright has unwittingly been infringed.

The views expressed in this work are those
of the authors and do not necessarily reflect
those of the National Examining Board for
Supervision and Management or of the publisher.

NEBS Management Project Manager: Diana Thomas
Author: Joe Johnson
Editor: Diana Thomas
Series Editor: Diana Thomas
Based on previous material by: Joe Johnson
Composition by Genesis Typesetting, Rochester, Kent
Printed and bound in Great Britain

Workbook introduction

Here are the workbook titles in each module which link with *Motivating People*, should you wish to extend your study to other Super Series workbooks. There is a brief description of each workbook in the User Guide.

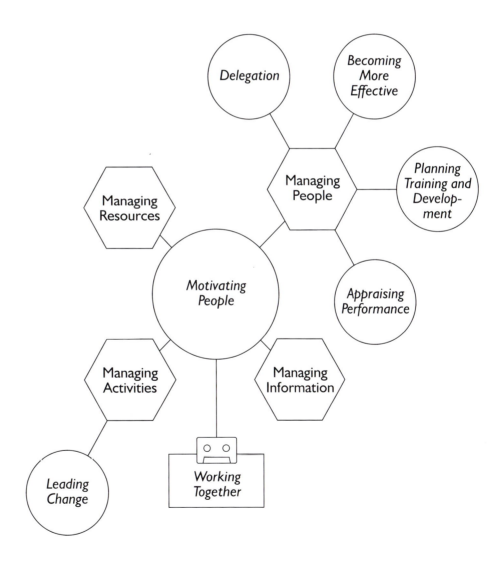

2 S/NVQ links

This workbook relates to the following elements:

C9.1 Contribute to the identification of development needs
C9.2 Contribute to planning the development of teams and individuals
C9.4 Contribute to the assessment of people against development objectives
C12.3 Provide feedback to teams and individuals on their work.

It will also help you to develop the following Personal Competences:

- building teams;
- relating and showing sensitivity to others.

3 Workbook objectives

One of the most commonly asked questions by managers, in all walks of life, is:

How can I get my staff to be more highly motivated – more concerned and involved with what we're trying to achieve?

There is, unfortunately, no simple answer to this kind of question, no technique or stratagem that can be universally applied.

> '... although the field of motivation is concerned with the regulation and change of behaviour, it goes deeper to consider the very nature of human beings.' – Edward L. Deci, *The History of Motivation in Psychology and Its Relevance for Management.*

The problem is that people are too complicated, and too diverse in their nature and qualities. What will make one person behave positively may have the opposite effect on the next individual.

Nevertheless, there are approaches that do seem to work, at least for most people, most of the time. And the better you get to know the particular people you are working with, the better you will be able to understand their wants, their needs, and what drives them.

This workbook has four sessions. The first is brief; it defines terms and sets the scene. Session B consists of a review of 'classical' theory about motivation, some of it going back over 50 years. The subject is treated from several points of view: the needs of human beings (Maslow); an examination of the attitudes managers have towards employees (McGregor); motivation and 'maintenance' factors (Herzberg); the links between rewards and motivation; 'internal' motivation (Hackman and Oldham). All this theory may seem daunting, but you should not find it too difficult to follow. The intention is that by the end of the session you will have a good grasp of a number of principles that can be applied in the workplace.

In Session C, our focus is mainly on 'job enrichment' – ways to make work more satisfying and intrinsically rewarding. This draws on much of the theory of the previous session. Finally, in Session D, we look at motivation of the team, as seen from the team leader's point of view.

3.1 Objectives

At the end of this workbook you should be **better able to**:

- identify some of the factors which tend to motivate and those which do not;
- understand the behaviour of the people you work with;
- put into effect the principles of job enrichment;
- find ways of motivating the members of your workteam.

4 Activity planner

Portfolio of evidence

If you are compiling an S/NVQ portfolio, you might like to develop some of the activities in this workbook as evidence of your competence. Particular activities you may want to take a look at in advance are those in Session D, i.e., Activities 38 (page 64), 40 (page 67) and 41 (page 68) and the Work-based assignment. These may provide the basis of evidence for an S/NVQ portfolio. All Portfolio Activities and the Work-based assignment are signposted with the portfolio icon shown on the left of this page. The icon states the elements to which the Portfolio Activities and Work-based assignment relate.

The Work-based assignment (on page 74) asks you to select a job you feel would benefit from job enrichment, and to develop a plan to achieve this. This can also be used for your portfolio of evidence and should be useful in helping to demonstrate your competence in ensuring that such a plan:

- is consistent with team objectives and organizational values;
- reflects the identified training and development needs of all personnel for whom you have responsibility;
- is clear, relevant, realistic and takes account of team and organizational constraints;
- is agreed with individual team members and takes account of their work activities, learning ability and personal circumstances.

Session A What is motivation?

1 Introduction

'How many articles, books, speeches, and workshops have pleaded plaintively, "How do I get an employee to do what I want him to do?"

In lectures to industry on the problem, I have found that the audiences are anxious for quick and practical answers, so I will begin with a straightforward, practical formula for moving people. The surest and least circumlocuted way of getting someone to do something is to kick him in the pants – give him what might be called the KITA.'

Frederick Herzberg, *One More Time: How Do You Motivate Employees?*

In case you are wondering whether to take these comments seriously, Frederick Herzberg went on to explain that kicking people may be one way to move them, but it is definitely **not** motivation.

Well, what is motivation? What exactly does the word mean, and why is it important to managers? How does it affect the behaviour of individuals? And to what extent is the success of organizations dependent upon the motivation of employees?

These are some of the questions we will start to look at in this session, although not all the answers will become clear until later in the workbook.

To begin with, we define the word motivation and relate it to the aims and functions of managers. Then we will look at values, attitudes and atmosphere. This session should prepare you for the theories of motivation covered in Session B.

2 Definitions

Management tends to be all things to all people so we will start by gaining some agreement about what we **do** mean.

Activity 1

3 mins

How do you see your primary role as manager? Tick the one sentence below which you would you say **best** describes your **main** function as a manager.

a   To get a job done. ☐

b   To organize and control your team so that the job which management has defined is completed satisfactorily. ☐

c   To get your team to perform a task which meets the objectives of the organization. ☐

d   To make it possible for the team members to get the most satisfaction from their work. ☐

e   To lead your team so that defined objectives are reached and the task is carried out to the best possible ability of the team. ☐

Your response depends on how you see your role and how it has been defined for you. However, I think that:

a   'To get a job done' is too simple a definition, and suggests you do the work yourself, rather than the team doing it.

b   'To organize and control your team so that the job which management has defined is completed satisfactorily' is, on the face of things, acceptable. Organizing and controlling is frequently considered part of a manager's job. But for many teams and team leaders, 'control' is not always an appropriate word, because many teams control their own activities to a large extent. In today's working world, the manager is expected to take a less authoritarian role. As we will discuss later, this can have positive motivating effects.

   In any case, this description is inadequate on the grounds that management is not usually just a question of completing a job satisfactorily. A good front-line manager would have higher ambitions than that.

c   'To get your team to perform a task which meets the objectives of the organization' would certainly be close. Again though, this definition doesn't go far enough, in my opinion.

d   'To make it possible for the team members to get the most satisfaction from their work' is surely wrong – you aren't paid primarily to keep the team satisfied, though that may be a secondary objective.

e   I think that 'To lead your team so that defined objectives are reached and the task is carried out to the best possible ability of the team' is the best answer. Most managers are expected to achieve the best possible results. and to get the best from the team.

In the MCI Management Standards 'the key purpose of management' is expressed as: 'To achieve the organization's objectives and continuously improve its performance.'

2

This Activity leads us nearer to the subject of this workbook: getting the best from the team while achieving defined objectives.

So, when there is a job to be done, how can you, the manager, get your team to do it?

You can select people who have the necessary skills and knowledge to do the job efficiently. If the required attributes are lacking, you can train team members to acquire the skills, or you can try to design jobs so that they are compatible with the team's existing abilities. But finding ways to match people to jobs is not enough. The other factor, which will be critical in determining **how well** the job gets done, is the **motivation** of those doing the work.

There are lots of ways of getting people to carry out tasks to a desired performance level, of course.

Activity 2

4 mins

Suppose you have a job to complete which is nearing its deadline. You need that extra effort from the team if the objective is to be reached in time. The problem is to persuade the members to concentrate that little bit harder, to make that additional endeavour.

For this situation, write down four or five different possible actions you might take. Don't worry whether you think a particular action would be successful. For instance, one action might be to beat them all with a stick until they agreed to work harder.

_____

_____

_____

_____

_____

_____

There are lots of options open to you. You could:

- use force – the KITA, perhaps;
- shout at them;
- plead with them;
- coax them by gentle persuasion;
- praise their performance so far;
- appeal to their better nature;
- stress the importance of the job;

- try to make the job more enjoyable;
- remind them of their duty;
- promise rewards – like buying them a drink;
- threaten them;
- let them know the probable results of **not** doing what you want them to, and leave them to make up their own minds.

These are only some of the possible actions you might take.

Determining which, if any, of these methods will be successful requires an understanding of human beings in general, and of those team members in particular.

2.1 Motivation

Now let's try to define the word 'motivation'. Perhaps you'd like to start by writing down your own definition.

Activity 3

3 mins

Write down, briefly, what the word 'motivation' means to you.

_____

_____

_____

_____

Your answer may be included in those below. Motivation:

- means getting someone to do what you want them to do;
- is what makes us want to do something;
- is a kind of driving force which comes from within;
- is needed when we have a desire to achieve some objective;
- is an incentive to cause us to try to do something.

All these are more or less correct. Motivation has a lot to do with incentive and desire. It does **not** have much to do with threats, violence or seduction. When we say we're motivated to do something, we don't mean that we're being **made** to do it, or that we're being **enticed** to do it. We mean we **want** to do it.

To motivate somebody to do something, you have to get them to want to do it.

> 'I have a year-old Schnauzer. When it was a small puppy and I wanted it to move, I kicked it in the rear and it moved. Now that I have finished its obedience training, I hold up a dog biscuit when I want the Schnauzer to move. . . . I am the one who is motivated, and the dog is the one who moves. In this instance all I did was apply KITA frontally: I exerted a pull instead of a push' – Frederick Herzberg, *One More Time: How Do You Motivate Employees?*

A definition of motivation from the *Longman Dictionary of the English Language* is: 'A conscious or unconscious driving force that arouses and directs action towards the achievement of a desired goal.'

If we accept this definition, it gives us several things to think about:

- motivation can be conscious or unconscious, so we aren't necessarily aware of what it is that motivates us;
- motivation is a driving force, and is therefore a powerful influence – for good or ill;
- a motivating factor will 'arouse and direct action'. This suggests that, once a person is motivated, he or she will be driven to act in a certain way. If the motivation is strong, it may not always be easy to direct and supervise these actions from outside;
- another difficulty in a work situation may be to make the 'desired goal' coincide with the goal of the organization.

Let's look now at what does, or does not, motivate different people.

3 Values and attitudes

- Rula Myers turned out for her club hockey team every week. She enjoyed playing and regarded it as a good form of exercise, but hockey wasn't really an important part of her life.

  Then Rula was offered the job of Club Captain. When she accepted, she completely changed her attitude. She gave up a lot more of her spare time in order to organize matches and functions, and on the field she was like a girl inspired, becoming top goal scorer. Rula was very popular. The club had its best season ever.

- Manny Tarbuck liked his job as crane operator. He enjoyed being able to manipulate and control the machinery in a very precise way. When he went home in the evening though, he forgot about work.

  Then Manny was given a new job, training new people to operate the cranes. This didn't suit him at all. He got annoyed with recruits who didn't quickly get the hang of things, or who didn't work as hard as he did. And he went home at night still worrying about the job and wishing he could go back to being an operator himself.

5

■ Drew Winterton and his manager Naomi got on very well together. Drew hadn't been in the job very long and would sometimes get into difficulties. When that happened, Naomi would sit down and talk to him, asking him where he thought he had gone wrong. She wouldn't tell him what to do, but would try to get Drew to explain his own mistakes. Most of the time, he would realise how to put things right. Then Drew went back to work determined to do a better job.

When Naomi was moved to another section, a new manager took over. This man was much more direct. If Drew came to him to ask for help, he would be told: 'Look, this is how you do it – OK?' Drew would nod and walk away, feeling like an idiot. He would go back to work looking at the clock and counting the minutes to the end of the shift.

> '... there is no "right" theory of motivation, but only the individual and the particular circumstances.' – Charles B. Handy *Understanding Organizations.*

What can we learn from these examples?

In the first, Rula reacted very positively to increased responsibility: it provided her with a motivation she hadn't had before. People often surprise us with their abilities when they're given the scope to express themselves.

In the second, Manny disliked the new job given to him and would have preferred to stay where he was. Just because someone is good at a job, it doesn't mean that he or she will be good at teaching others. To get the best from people we have to develop their natural talents.

In the third situation, Drew felt he could ask Naomi for help while still retaining his pride and independence. He wanted patient guidance and help, not brusquely given instructions.

These situations highlight some of the complexity of behaviour of human beings. In the same circumstances, other people may well have reacted differently. Our values – the things we see as important and desirable – vary a great deal from person to person.

Individuals may well regard differing things as motivating and demotivating in their work situation. (Something that is 'demotivating' has the opposite effect to something that is 'motivating'.) We can say that:

people aren't all motivated – or demotivated – by the same things.

And yet, as we will see later in the workbook, it **is** possible to identify a number of 'motivators' and 'demotivators' which tend to produce similar effects in most people.

Perhaps at this point you'd like to record some of your experiences of being motivated and demotivated. Understanding what motivates and demotivates you is a good start to understanding the behaviour and reactions of others.

Activity 4

10 mins

Think about some occasion in the past which made you feel very positive about your job. What happened at work to make you feel this way?

_____

_____

_____

_____

_____

Now try to think of some event which caused you to feel dissatisfied and rather negative about work.

_____

_____

_____

_____

_____

Your first answer – something which made you feel positive – may have been one of the following:

- a promotion;
- a pay increase;
- a 'thank you' or pat on the back from your manager for a job well done;
- the achievement of a target by your team;
- just the satisfaction of having accomplished something you had been striving for.

These things have the same effect on most of us, although being promoted may not be seen by everyone as desirable.

It's very likely, too, that the boost to your morale in getting a pay rise didn't last very long: most people quickly seem to get used to the idea of having more money in their pockets.

What made you feel negative? Was it one of the following?

- The frustration of not achieving something?
- A loss of responsibility?
- A disagreement with your manager or with a colleague?
- Some company rule or policy that you didn't agree with?
- A threat to your job status or security?

What is certain is that the people responding to this Activity will produce a great variety of answers. Managers need to be aware that

values and attitudes to work vary a great deal.

4 The right atmosphere

One thing that does affect everyone is the ambience or atmosphere in the workplace.

Activity 5

5 mins

Give your own organization and workplace marks out of ten for the following indicators of atmosphere.

In your opinion, to what extent: Marks out of 10
(10 is perfection)

- are people generally supportive and co-operative?
- is there an atmosphere of general good humour?
- do people tend to communicate well at and between all levels?
- is there mutual trust between most groups and most people?
- do managers have an open door policy?
- are people encouraged to develop their abilities?
- are decisions and information shared?
- is absenteeism and staff turnover low?
- is the accident frequency low?
- are customer complaints low?

Total marks = _____ (out of 100)

Your responses will reflect the 'atmosphere' of your workplace. Rate your workplace according to the table:

0 to 30	You obviously think the atmosphere is pretty poor. If others agree with you, you have a good deal to worry about.	The lower the rating, the more there is for you and the other managers to do. Start by reading the rest of this workbook!
31 to 60	Looks like there's a lot of room for improvement.	
61 to 80	A rating at this level means that, while you feel things aren't too bad, they could be better.	
81 to 100	This is excellent. You must believe it's a good place to work.	

An open, sharing atmosphere will tend to give people the scope to develop their skills and abilities. Organizations with such an atmosphere are more likely to have employees who identify with management objectives. In fact, they're more likely to succeed.

The atmosphere in the workplace is a key factor in motivating people.

We will return to this theme in the last session of the workbook.

Self-assessment 1

Fill in each blank in the following sentences with a suitable word, selected from the list below.

1 To _____ somebody to do something, you have to get them to _____ to do it.

2 Managers need to be aware that _____ and attitudes to work vary a great deal.

3 People aren't all motivated – or _____ – by the _____ things.

4 The _____ in the workplace is a _____ factor in motivating people.

ATMOSPHERE	DEMOTIVATED	KEY	MOTIVATE
SAME	VALUES	WANT	

9

(Questions 5 to 8). Tick those of the following statements that are **true**. Then explain briefly why they're true.

5 You can motivate people by threatening them with violence.   ☐

_____

_____

6 You can motivate people by promising them rewards.   ☐

_____

_____

7 Low absenteeism and high staff turnover are associated with a good atmosphere in an organization.   ☐

_____

_____

8 An open, sharing atmosphere will tend to give people the scope to develop their skills and abilities.   ☐

Answers to these questions can be found on page 81.

5 Summary

- Motivation has a lot to do with incentive and desire. It does **not** have much to do with threats, violence or seduction.

- To motivate somebody to do something, you have to get them to **want** to do it.

- A definition of motivation is: 'A conscious or unconscious driving force that arouses and directs action towards the achievement of a desired goal.'

- People aren't all motivated by the same things.

- The atmosphere in the workplace is a key factor in motivating people.

Session B Understanding behaviour at work

1 Introduction

Understanding what motivates people is usually quite difficult. There is no simple formula: you can't say 'treat people like this and you'll get the best from them'.

The subject has occupied many brilliant minds over the past fifty years or so. In the next few sections we are going to look at some of the most significant theories about the behaviour of people at work.

These are:

- Douglas McGregor's 'Theory X and Theory Y'.
- Abraham Maslow's theory of needs.
- Frederick Herzberg's 'two-factor' theory.
- Expectancy theory.
- Hackman and Oldham's essential job characteristics for internal motivation.

You may feel that this is a lot to take in. However, you aren't expected to remember the names, or even which theory is which. The important thing is to understand the ideas we discuss. Then in the remainder of the workbook we can use these ideas and see how far they can be applied to your kind of workplace.

2 Maslow: needs theory

2.1 Maslow's hierarchy of needs

'But what happens to man's desires when there is plenty of bread and when his belly is chronically filled? At once other (and 'higher') needs emerge and these, rather than physiological hungers, dominate the organism. And when these in turn are satisfied, again new (and still 'higher') needs emerge and so on.' — A. H. Maslow, *A Theory of Human Motivation* (1943).

What are the needs of human beings? What must they have in order to be happy, successful – or even just to survive?

The American psychologist Abraham Maslow considered these questions and came to the conclusion that human needs can be thought of as being on several distinct levels:

- **Physiological needs.** If we are starving or have other fundamental needs like air, sleep and water, we become obsessed with satisfying these needs. Anything else is irrelevant at this time.

- **Safety needs.** Once these bodily needs are satisfied, we look for security, and stability in our environment.

- **Love needs.** Having fed ourselves and made ourselves safe, the next level of need comes into play. The 'love' or social needs are then important to us – affection, friendship and belonging.

- **Esteem needs.** After satisfying all these 'lower' needs, we look for esteem, self-respect and achievement.

- **The need for self-actualization.** The final human goal is self-fulfilment – the development of our full potential in whatever field our talents lie.

EXTENSION I
You may like to read Maslow's work for yourself. If so, you will find a 13 page abridged version of Maslow's *A Theory of Human Motivation* in the book *Management and Motivation* edited by V. Vroom and E. Deci.

We can represent Maslow's ideas in the form of a staircase diagram:

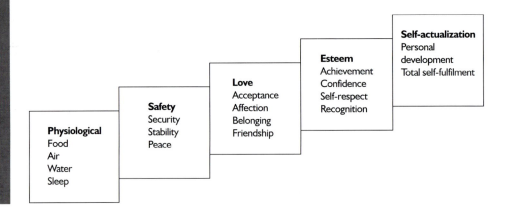

Activity 6

5 mins

State which of Maslow's 'needs categories' might be satisfied by each of the following items, by putting a tick in the appropriate column.

	Physiological	Safety	Love	Esteem	Self-actualization
A drinking fountain					
A feeling that you are attaining your career ambition.					
A comfortable working temperature.					
Meeting well the demands of your job.					
Being accepted as a valued member of a working group.					
Breathing equipment for a firefighter.					
Enjoying the respect of your manager.					

See whether you agree with my answers, which are given on page 84.

2.2 Some alternatives to Maslow's ideas

Since Maslow's work was published in the 1940s, people have looked again at the concept that human needs are arranged in a hierarchy.

In particular, Edward E. Lawler III claimed that the evidence supporting these ideas is not sufficiently convincing.

He suggested that some needs are always present, like the need for dignity and fair treatment. Other needs come and go, like hunger and the need for the company of others.

C. P. Alderfer simplified Maslow's list down to three categories:

- **existence**,
- **relating to others**, and
- **growth**.

Alderfer suggested that these three factors can operate at the same time. This rather contradicts Maslow's theory that people are aware of higher order needs only when lower order needs are satisfied.

He also put forward the idea that the less a need is fulfilled, the more important it becomes.

Answering the following questions may help you decide whether you think that Alderfer was right.

Activity 7

2 mins

If someone is out of work, struggling to support a family, are they still concerned about other needs such as self-respect and love?	YES	NO
If this state of affairs gets worse, so that the person is actually starving, do other needs diminish?	YES	NO
If a person feels lacking in love and friendship, can they still want to accomplish other things?	YES	NO

My views are that:

- if you are having a hard time, you don't completely forget about the need for self-respect; also, it may be love which makes you more determined to overcome the problems and to make your family better off;
- fortunately not many of us have experienced starvation, but we can imagine that, as such basic needs get stronger, other needs would seem to be less important;
- a person lacking in love and friendship may want to satisfy that need, but may still have time and ambition to accomplish other things.

In summary, it certainly seems true that more than one level of need can exist at the same time. In addition, I would say that when a need is recognized and cannot be fulfilled, it becomes more important.

My conclusion is, therefore, that Alderfer's ideas coincide with common experience.

Of course, people look to satisfy their needs in their life as a whole, not simply at work. For instance, some people have hobbies which fulfil all their higher needs; work seems to leave them quite untouched.

Nevertheless, in this workbook we are most concerned with motivation and work, so let's examine how theories about needs relate to the workplace.

2.3 Human needs and the workplace

Because most people spend so much of their lives at work, it is important to recognize that they may regard it as more than simply a means of earning money. In fact, of course, people in voluntary teams may not get paid at all, and yet are still motivated to perform work.

Activity 8

4 mins

Think of yourself or a member of your team. In your view, which of the following 'needs' does this person have which are (at least partially) fulfilled by working?

The need to survive. ☐

The need to interact with other human beings. ☐

The need to feel secure. ☐

The need to feel accepted by others. ☐

The need to satisfy a desire to live a fuller life by helping others. ☐

The need for self-respect and a sense of achievement that comes from doing something worthwhile. ☐

The need to be recognized for accomplishments, efforts, skills and abilities. ☐

The need to develop as a human being. ☐

The usual reason why people go to work at all is to earn enough money to live – assuming they get paid for what they do. But once their income is sufficient to support them, most people look for other kinds of benefits. These aren't always tangible and may include all those things listed above.

■ The need to survive is the most common reason most people go to work in the first place. Work brings the money to buy food and clothes, and to house ourselves.

- The need to interact with other human beings is often satisfied by going to work. Indeed, for some people, relationships with others is the most important thing. Being a member of a team, or working with patients, those in need, or with customers, is often a very rewarding experience. Acceptance by others is a need which is closely allied to this.

- The need to satisfy a desire to live a fuller life by helping others is clearly a motivating factor for some, and may override all other considerations.

- Work often fulfils the security needs of people to some extent. Certainly the opposite seems to be true – when a person is out of paid employment, he or she may feel very insecure.

- Self-respect and a sense of achievement also seem to be very real needs. The extent to which they are fulfilled by work depends on the work being done: some work may be very unfulfilling in this respect.

- Most of us seek recognition for our skills and abilities as well as for our accomplishments and our efforts. As we spend so much time at work, it is not surprising to find that for many people this need is satisfied only through work.

- Many would say that the need to develop as a human being is every bit as strong as the need for, say, food and drink. Again, the amount of time we spend at work means that we look upon our work to help us satisfy this need.

3 McGregor: Theory X and Theory Y

How do managers see the behaviour of people at work?

Douglas McGregor believed that managerial decisions and actions were based on the assumptions they made about human nature and human behaviour. He wrote about his ideas in his book *The Human Side of Enterprise*.

EXTENSION 2
Extracts from McGregor's book, *The Human Side of Enterprise*, summarizing the main points, can be found in *Management and Motivation*, which is listed as one of our extensions on page 79.

McGregor suggested that managerial strategy was greatly influenced by a view of human nature which assumes that:

- people inherently dislike work and will avoid it if they can;
- because they dislike work they have to be offered rewards to work, and threatened with punishment if they don't;
- they prefer to be controlled and directed, want to avoid responsibility, have little ambition and desire security more than anything else.

McGregor labelled this set of assumptions **Theory X**.

Activity 9

2 mins

What do you think about Theory X? Glance again at the three ideas you have just read.

a Do you think these ideas are an accurate description of people at work?

YES NO

b Do you think that managers frequently have such views of people at work?

YES NO

'People today are accustomed to being directed, manipulated, controlled in industrial organizations and to finding satisfaction for their social, egoistic and self-fulfillment needs away from the job. This is true of much of management as well of workers.' — McGregor, writing in 1957.

McGregor wrote his views in the 1950s, and they were observations of American industry. Nevertheless, you may agree with me that some managers in Britain today still seem to act as if they believed that the ideas listed in Theory X were a good description of their employees' behaviour. Fortunately, this kind of manager is less in evidence these days, as companies adopt more enlightened views. (Or perhaps you don't agree!)

I don't think that the ideas set out in Theory X are valid, in the sense of being useful and leading to high levels of motivation, and of course McGregor didn't think so either.

McGregor fully accepted the human needs levels idea that we discussed when talking about Abraham Maslow. He went on to say that, when times were very difficult, such as in a depression, a strategy based on Theory X may be workable. When people are concerned about satisfying their needs for food and security, then they would be more likely to respond to the 'stick and carrot' approach which is suggested by Theory X.

However, according to McGregor, when we aren't living in such extreme conditions, management strategies based on these ideas lead to dissatisfaction and conflict. He thought that people needed much more from work than wages and security.

He felt that in fact, given the chance, people at work would behave quite differently from the expectations set out in Theory X. McGregor wrote down these more discerning views and labelled them **Theory Y**:

- people do not dislike work, and under the right conditions they can enjoy it;
- if they are committed to the objectives of the group, they will direct and control themselves, rather than having to be controlled from above;
- people will be committed to objectives if they are getting enough personal satisfaction from the job;
- the average human being learns to accept and to seek responsibility, if the conditions are right;
- ingenuity and creativity are widely distributed and generally under-utilized;

These are very different ideas to Theory X, aren't they? McGregor saw them as being 'dynamic rather than static; they indicate the possibility of human growth, and development'.

17

Activity 10

4
mins

You may like to give your opinions of Theory Y. Glance again at the five ideas you have just read.

Do you believe that people at work behave like this – or might behave like this if they were given the opportunity?

_____

_____

_____

_____

_____

I don't know how you may have answered this Activity. I imagine there might be a range of responses, such as:

- 'Yes, this is exactly right. This is how people would behave if only employers would let them!'
- 'Some people might behave like this, but I don't think all of them do. A lot of people I know behave more like Theory X'
- 'I accept some of the ideas of Theory Y, but not all of them.'

Even Douglas McGregor himself accepted that his ideas may in time prove to be wrong; that's why he called them theories. Theory Y does seem to have stood the test of time, nevertheless. They are seen today by many people as being perfectly valid.

Later on in the workbook we will refer back to Theory X and Theory Y when we are discussing other ideas. For the moment, I'll just remind you once more what the two theories comprise:

Theory X

- People inherently dislike work and will avoid it if they can.

- Because they dislike work they have to be offered rewards to work, and threatened with punishment if they don't.

- They prefer to be controlled and directed, want to avoid responsibility, have little ambition and desire security more than anything else.

> **Theory Y**
>
> - People do not dislike work; under the right conditions they can enjoy it.
> - If they are committed to the objectives of the group, they will direct and control themselves, rather than having to be controlled from above.
> - People will be committed to objectives if they are getting enough personal satisfaction from the job.
> - The average human being learns to accept and to seek responsibility, if the conditions are right.
> - Ingenuity and creativity are widely distributed and generally under-utilized.

4 Herzberg: the two-factor theory

Many people have found Herzberg's exploration of motivation gives them a useful insight into how people feel about their work.

Activity 11

2 mins

Without thinking about it too much, would you say that the things that motivate people are the opposite of the things that demotivate them?

YES   NO

You may well have said 'Yes'; many people would probably give this response. It might be argued, for example, that a wage increase would be motivating, while a decrease would be demotivating. Or if a pat on the back gives us a good feeling, a reprimand could make us feel bad.

Frederick Herzberg, another American Professor of Psychology, did some investigation into this subject. He asked 200 accountants and engineers to describe those times when they felt **exceptionally good** about their jobs and those times when they felt **exceptionally bad** about them.

His analysis showed that what caused the good feelings were **not** the opposite to what caused bad feelings – they were completely **different** factors. These results were repeated in further studies involving men and women from a variety of occupations in America and Europe.

Herzberg came to the conclusion that

the factors producing job satisfaction are quite different from the factors that lead to job dissatisfaction.

19

4.1 The motivating factors

Herzberg said that the five factors 'which stand out as strong determiners of job satisfaction' are

- achievement;
- recognition;
- work itself;
- responsibility;
- advancement;

As you read my summaries of these ideas, try to decide for yourself whether you feel that what Herzberg said seems right to you.

- **Achievement**

The personal satisfaction of completing a job, solving its problems and seeing the successful results of your own efforts.

- **Recognition**

The acknowledgement for a job efficiently done. This may arise from within the individual or be appreciation shown by others.

- **Work itself**

The positive effects of the job upon the person. The job may, for example, be interesting, varied, creative and challenging.

- **Responsibility**

The degree of control a person has over the work. The amount of control that people can exercise is, in part, influenced by their authority and the responsibility that goes with it.

- **Advancement**

The opportunity to achieve promotion within the organisation. Advancement also occurs when someone is given more freedom to exercise initiative in their normal work.

Activity 12

Now answer the following questions, to see how far you agree that each of these are motivating factors.

a When you have completed a difficult job to your own satisfaction, and can see the effects of what you have done, does it make you feel more positive about work? | YES | NO |

b If your manager compliments you on some aspect of your work, does it usually make you feel as if you want to do even better? | YES | NO |

c Do you feel more motivated when you are enjoying your work, than when you find it boring or unpleasant? | YES | NO |

d If you feel that you are in control of, and responsible for, what you are doing, does this make you better motivated to do a good job? | YES | NO |

e Are you motivated by the possibility of promotion, or of moving on to more interesting or more rewarding work? | YES | NO |

If you answered YES, without qualification, to all these questions, then you probably agree with Herzberg's list of motivating factors.

If you didn't simply answer YES, then you disagree to some extent. There's certainly no harm in disagreeing. As you have probably realized by now, there are no hard and fast rules about this subject. In fact, it isn't a question of following a set of rules at all. How you apply motivation in your job will depend on your own understanding of the way people behave.

4.2 The maintenance factors

The factors which Herzberg found to have the effect of causing dissatisfaction, but which do not affect motivation in any positive way, are called **maintenance** factors. Another phrase that Herzberg used was 'hygiene factors'.

Maintenance factors can reduce the level of performance but not increase it. The analogy is that lack of maintenance may cause equipment to deteriorate, but regular maintenance will not improve its performance.

Activity 13

3 mins

Imagine you are happy with the job your team is doing. Working conditions are quite good. Then you learn that the building where you work has got to undergo a lot of alteration. Unfortunately, there is nowhere else for you to go and the builders have to work around your team members while they are trying to do their work. During this period tempers are frayed, absenteeism increases and output goes down. Once the building work is finished, however, things go back to normal. Output is back to its previous levels. Working conditions are better than before, although this does not have any noticeable effect on performance.

What conclusions might you draw about the effects of working conditions on performance?

_____

_____

_____

_____

_____

The maintenance factors are:

- working conditions;
- policy and admin;
- interpersonal relationships;
- salary or wages;
- status;
- job security.

You might reasonably conclude that working conditions don't affect the performance of the team, **provided** that they are fairly good. If the conditions become very difficult, performance **is** affected – adversely. If on the other hand working conditions become better than just **quite good,** it makes little difference to performance.

This was just the sort of result that Herzberg found. **Working conditions** is one of the maintenance factors.

I'll go through Herzberg's other maintenance factors now. This time, I'll ask you to think about each one as we come to it.

- **Company (or organizational) policy and administration**

This means the overall operation of the organization – how it is managed and organized. If company policies conflict with the aims of groups or individuals, for example, negative consequences will result.

Activity 14

Can you recall an occasion when a company decision or policy upset you or one of your workteam? If you can, describe it very briefly.

_____

_____

Do you think that lack of these kind of problems makes people better motivated?

_____

_____

It is a common experience for employees to feel upset by some policy or decision made elsewhere in the company. Often, this is simply because, although the decision may be made for the good of the whole organization, some people aren't told the reason for it, even though they may be affected.

My view is that this rings true – that company policy and administration can act in a demotivating way, but that when employees don't feel affected by such things they don't think about them.

You may feel that the next of Herzberg's maintenance factors is more controversial.

■ **Supervision**.

The accessibility, and social and technical competence of the manager.

Activity 15

What about this one? How much are people affected by the performance of their manager – is it a maintenance factor or a motivating one? In thinking about this question, you might like to distinguish between the supervision of one person and the supervision of a team. Perhaps you could compare the relationships between you and your manager, and between your team and you.

After you've given it some thought, jot down your views in the space below.

_____

_____

_____

_____

As I said, I think that the question of whether supervision is a maintenance factor is more debatable.

Other experts have disagreed with Herzberg here. Leadership plays a very important role in motivation, especially the motivation of a team.

It may be true that you find that you – as an individual, rather than one of a team – don't spend much time thinking about your manager, until he or she is not available (or is giving you a hard time!) You may feel that you don't regard your relationship with your manager as a significant motivating factor.

Even if this is true, I wonder if the same can be said of your team's relationship with you. A workteam depends on a team leader to a far greater extent, as a rule.

I don't think we can come to any firm conclusions here. Perhaps you might like to think about it some more, or discuss the question with a colleague.

The next maintenance factor, according to Herzberg, is:

■ **Interpersonal relations**

The quality of the relationships between members of the team. When they are bad, they may interfere with work; when they are good – or at least acceptable – they don't make any significant difference to behaviour.

Activity 16

4 mins

To test whether you agree with this as a maintenance factor, try to recall an occasion when two team members clashed. What was the effect on their work?

_____

_____

_____

Then ask yourself whether, when people 'get along OK', they are motivated better.

_____

_____

_____

It may have not been difficult to remember an incident when conflict between people affected performance in a negative way. Perhaps we can agree that, when the quality of relationships is poor, people may become demotivated.

When it comes to good relationships, you may think that this can act in a very positive way. We've already discussed the fact that the human needs for interaction with, and acceptance by, others are very real. To what extent good relationships are motivating is again a question for debate.

Another of Herzberg's maintenance factors is:

■ **Salary**

The income of individuals. The surprising finding of Herzberg is that wages or salary does not generally motivate people while they are doing the job, although lack of it does demotivate.

It was once thought that pay was the main motivating factor. Writing in 1911, Frederick W. Taylor said:

'. . . it is impossible, through any long period of time, to get workmen to work much harder than the average men around them, unless they are assured a large and permanent increase in their pay.'

> When you hear people say: 'So long as they keep paying me, I'm happy', then you know they aren't happy. True or false?

Activity 17

3 mins

Say whether you agree with Taylor's statement, and briefly explain your reasoning.

_____

_____

_____

_____

This is another issue which is not very straightforward. Financial reward is the main reason why most people work. But, if we are engrossed in our work and enjoy it, we may not give salary a moment's thought throughout our working day.

Pay is certainly not the only thing that motivates. However, it does become extremely important when we feel that we are underpaid – or if the company forgets to pay us! We may then feel very negative about work. If this is true, then it seems that Herzberg is right – money is a maintenance factor.

But suppose your company decides to pay your team a bonus, which is directly dependent on output or performance. Here, money is being used as a motivator.

Also, the differentials of salary may become more important than the amount of money being paid. People often seem to worry more about their earnings compared with the next person, rather than their actual salary level. Studies have shown that managers typically will believe that people above and below them are overpaid, while they themselves are underpaid. This kind of belief has a demotivating effect.

This aspect of salary brings us to the next of Herzberg's maintenance factors:

■ **Status**

This is an individual's position in relation to others. Status 'symbols', such as title, are important. A perceived reduction in status can be very demoralizing.

Activity 18

■ Think back to the day when you were promoted to your present position. If you are honest, did you feel a little elated with your new status?

| YES | NO |

■ Now you are used to the idea, is the fact of your status important to your motivation to work?

| YES | NO |

■ If tomorrow you were demoted, so that you were no longer a manager, would this have a demotivating effect?

| YES | NO |

If you answered YES – NO – YES (in that order) to the questions in this Activity, then you probably agree that status is a maintenance factor, not a motivating one.

Even if you have doubts about this, perhaps you would be more ready to concede the last of the Herzberg maintenance factors:

■ **Job security.**

Freedom from concern about keeping a job.

I think there is less room for argument here. I would say that most people are not normally motivated by the fact of having a job, but may become very demotivated should there be a threat of losing it.

4.3 Conclusions and criticisms

Herzberg's motivating factors:

- achievement;
- responsibility;
- the work itself;
- recognition;
- advancement;

can all be said to be one's feelings about **the job itself**. As Herzberg wrote, the motivating factors:

'all seem to describe man's relationship to what he does: his job content, achievement on a task, recognition for task achievement, the nature of the task, responsibility for a task and professional advancement or growth in task capability.'

Conversely, the maintenance factors:

- working conditions
- company policy and administration
- interpersonal relations
- salary
- status
- job security

can all be said to do with **the working environment**. Herzberg said of these that:

'... the "dissatisfier" factors describe his relationship to the context or environment in which he does his job.'

Thus the first group of factors are relevant to the work a person does and the other to the environment in which it is done.

Or:

the causes of satisfaction at work lie in the content of the job; the causes of dissatisfaction lie in the working environment.

Herzberg's findings were very significant for managers. They drew attention to the fact that job content has a great influence on the behaviour of people at work, and that factors like salary and working conditions may not in themselves motivate.

However, Herzberg does have his critics.

Part of this criticism is related to Herzberg's claim that by building motivators into the job, people at work will experience job **satisfaction**.

The question is: does job satisfaction lead to high performance?

Perhaps you have your own views.

> Is this all a bit too simplistic? What do you think?

Activity 19

2 mins

Do you think that a satisfied workteam is a productive one?

Think about this for a few minutes and then tick the appropriate box.

| YES | NO | NOT SURE |

Common sense would suggest that job satisfaction and productivity go hand in hand. Yet at the same time it is difficult to argue with the following statement from *Human Resources Management* by H. T. Graham (1994), Pitman.

'It is possible for any degree of job satisfaction to be associated with any degree of productivity, that is, a satisfied worker may have low productivity or a dissatisfied worker may have high productivity, or vice versa.'

So it would appear that although a satisfied workteam **can** be productive, it is not necessarily so.

There is no doubt that Herzberg's work has had a great deal of impact and has caused people to question traditional values. Even if you don't agree with all his findings, I hope this short synopsis has given you plenty of food for thought.

As we go through the workbook, we will refer back to Herzberg's theories.

5 Expectancy

EXTENSION 3
An article by Edward E. Lawler III, entitled 'Job design and employee motivation' is reproduced in the book *Management and Motivation*. It is relevant to the subject and you may care to treat it as background reading. It is nine pages long.

In this section we will look at some wider aspects of motivation.

What I am going to describe comes under the general heading of 'Expectancy Theory'.

The reason for trying to motivate people at work is, as we've already discussed, because motivated employees are more likely to want to achieve the objectives which managers have set. Another way of saying this is that when **motivation** is high, improved **performance** usually results.

But of course, improved performance only comes about through the **efforts** of the motivated workers.

So we can say that

| Motivation | results in | Effort | which leads to improved | Performance |

What provides the motivation? It may be one of many things. (According to Herzberg, if you recall, it can be achievement, recognition, the work itself, responsibility or advancement.) If we are looking for one word which sums up what motivates people, a word which seems appropriate is REWARD – the reward of achieving something, the reward of recognition, and so on.

So we can now complete our diagram:

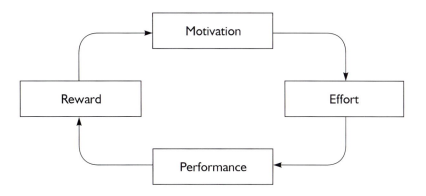

As you can see,

Motivation   depends upon   Reward
Reward   depends upon   Performance
Performance   depends upon   Effort
Effort   depends upon   Motivation

Let's look at a particular incident, and then try to work out how this motivation–effort–performance–reward cycle applies to a real life situation.

■ Sean Gale was the manager in charge of a team of machine operators in a modern clothing factory. The machines were semi-automatic, and the rate of production depended as much on the operator as the machine. The work needed a lot of concentration, and it was easy to spoil material by not keeping one's mind on the job.

Sean's manager called him in one day and told him: 'Sean, we have a new contract, which means we will have to increase production, to keep up with the orders. Unfortunately, as this is a one-off contract, we can't afford to bring in more machinery. How do we get your team to step up their work-rate?'

Sean's reaction was immediate. 'We have to offer them a bonus. There's no other way in the short term'.

Sean's manager then agreed a bonus of 5 per cent of weekly wages, provided the production work-rate was increased by 10 per cent.

Activity 20

The company wanted the team to make an extra **effort**, so that **performance** would improve, and output would go up. To encourage this effort, it was prepared to offer a **reward** in terms of a bonus.

When Sean leaves his manager's office, he has to tell the team about the plan. This is one point where the plan might go wrong.

When Sean talks to his team after seeing the manager, can you think of one thing that might go wrong, which could prevent the company's plan from succeeding?

_____

_____

_____

_____

_____

One thing that might go wrong is that the team may not consider the **reward** sufficient **motivation**, and so would not think it worthwhile making the extra effort being asked for.

Another is that, when Sean tells them about the plan, although its members are happy with the bonus offered, they believe that the increased production rate being demanded by the company is unrealistic. If the target set for achieving the reward is seen as being too high, the team members may decide that there is no point in trying to achieve it.

This is one place where the motivation–effort–performance–reward cycle might break down: between **reward** and **motivation**.

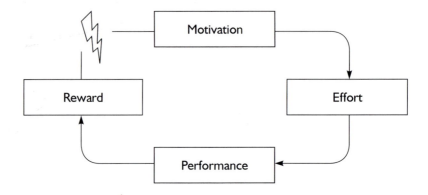

Let's continue the story of the clothing factory.

■ In fact, the production team accepted the proposed bonus, and agreed to step up production. So far so good.

However, the increased production was not achieved during the first week.

Activity 21

The plan did not break down at the reward–motivation stage, yet the required increase in production did not take place during the first week. Can you think of **two** things that might have gone wrong, to prevent the company plan working straight away?

_____

_____

_____

_____

You might have suggested that perhaps:

■ there was a shortage of materials, so that the operators couldn't increase production;
■ one or more of the machines went faulty, so that the operators on these machines had to stop work;
■ somebody went sick;
■ some of the team members weren't trained or experienced enough to increase their rate of production;
■ there was an accident, and a machine had to be switched off.

You may have thought of other possible reasons for the desired increase in production not being achieved.

Whatever the reason, the effect is a breakdown in the motivation–effort–performance part of the cycle. Either something prevents the effort being made, in spite of the fact that the team is motivated to improve performance, or the effort **is** made, but this does not result in better performance.

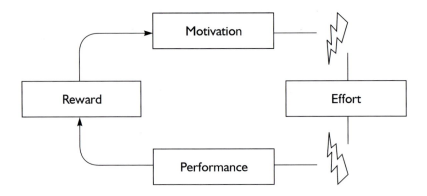

It is in this part of the cycle where the manager plays his or her most significant role. Often front-line managers have little say in the rewards being offered, especially monetary rewards.

Activity 22

3 mins

What could Sean do to try to make sure that the plan didn't break down at the motivation–effort–performance part of the cycle? Try to suggest **three** things he might do.

_____

_____

_____

Sean might:

- try to make sure that all the necessary resources were in place: materials, working equipment, and so on;
- ensure that the team was sufficiently well trained before asking them to step up the work rate;
- be especially alert in case of accidents, because it's often when the team are under extra pressure that accidents occur;
- make sure that the technicians who serviced machines were aware of the situation, so they could be ready to deal with breakdowns;
- check to see that other groups were geared up to handle increased output – for instance, inspectors and packers; there would be no point in stepping up production to meet an order if the finished products did not leave the factory in time.

It's quite possible that you thought of other suggestions. The real point is that motivating the team to improve performance is only one aspect of management and supervision, albeit an important one. To achieve the organization's objectives, many other factors have to be taken care of.

So far we've looked at two points where the motivation–effort–perform-ance–reward cycle could break down: at the reward–motivation stage and the motivation–effort–performance part of the cycle.

Can you think of one other part of the cycle where things could go wrong? Indicate your answer on the diagram below:

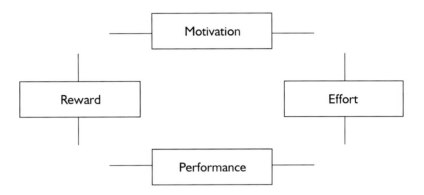

One other point in the cycle where things might go awry is at the performance–reward stage, so your diagram should have looked something like this:

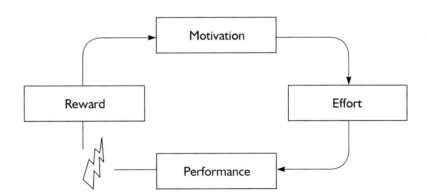

Suppose the team makes the effort to improve performance because they are motivated to do so by a promised or perceived reward. Then, for some reason, the reward does not materialize. How could this happen?

Perhaps:

- there is a dispute about whether the required workrate was achieved;
- the reward depends on other factors – such as a bonus being dependent on winning a certain sales order, which doesn't materialize;
- thinking of rewards other than money – the looked-for promotion may not be offered, or the effort not recognized.

So, in summary,

if motivation is to result in improved performance, every aspect of the motivation–effort–performance–reward cycle has to be considered.

6 Hackman and Oldham: internal motivation

J. Richard Hackman and Greg R. Oldham carried out research in the late 1970s. The work they subsequently published (in 1980) was based to some extent on the earlier theories we have discussed. However, they take a fresh approach.

Hackman and Oldham described a state of affairs in which people try to do well, because their work is rewarding and satisfying, as **internal motivation**. Their concept of the way this is achieved is shown in the following table:

The essential job characteristics:	What the worker gets from them:	The result, if all these job characteristics are present:
Feedback from job	→ Knowledge of the actual results of the work activities	
Autonomy	→ Experienced responsibility for outcomes of the work	High internal work motivation
Skill variety / Task identity / Task significance	→ Experienced meaningfulness of the work	

'Most people exhibit "motivational problems" at work when their tasks are designed so that they have little meaning, when they experience little responsibility for the work outcomes, or when they are protected from data about how well they are performing.' — J. Richard Hackman and Greg R. Oldham, 'Motivation Through the Design of Work' in Vroom and Deci, *Management and Motivation.*

All the essential job characteristics must be present, Hackman and Oldham said, for there to be high internal motivation. That is, every worker needs to have:

■ **feedback from the job;**

People ideally need clear information about the effectiveness of their performance, directly from the job. The emphasis here is on direct feedback, as when an actor hears the audience applaud, a doctor observes a patient responding to treatment, or someone painting white lines on a football pitch sees that they're straight and visible.

Feedback may also be provided through another agent, perhaps a manager or someone else, who makes an assessment about the person's work and passes it to the worker. This indirect feedback can be valuable, too.

Feedback provides **knowledge of the results** of the work. Workers, and teams, need to find out whether they are performing well or poorly.

■ **autonomy**;

The outcome of the job should be seen by workers to be substantially dependent on their own efforts, initiatives, and decisions.

Activity 24

2 mins

Suppose you perceive that a job that you're doing depends mainly on factors you cannot control: such as the company manual, your manager, or people in another work group. Are you more, or less likely to feel responsible for the results, than if you feel that you are the one in control of the work?

More likely	Less likely

Perhaps you believe that, as your autonomy – your control over the work – increases, you will tend to accept greater **responsibility for the results**. If so, I agree with you. People generally become more willing to be accountable for the success or failure of their efforts, and for the outcome, if they have a high level of autonomy.

■ **skill variety**;

This is the degree to which a job requires a variety of activities and skills. Workers who are able to perform tasks that they find challenging, and requiring more than one skill or ability, will experience meaningfulness. The more skills involved, the more meaningful the work is likely to be to them.

■ **task identity**;

Task identity is the extent to which a job requires a worker to finish a complete and identifiable piece of work, i.e., a task that has a beginning and end, and a visible outcome. People care about their work more when they are doing a whole job, rather than when their work overlaps with others in an undefined way. To take a simple case, if each member of a team of cleaners is given a specified area to clean, he or she is likely to find the work more meaningful than if the entire team works together on the whole area.

■ **task significance;**

This represents the amount of impact the job has on the lives of other people, whether those people are in the immediate organization or in the world at large. A nurse, who knows that the health of patients depends on his care, experiences a high degree of task significance. But if an inspector in a factory, say, is told nothing about those who subsequently sell, buy and use the product, he or she will experience low task significance.

These last three job characteristics – skill variety, task identity, and task significance – are essential if the worker is to **experience the work as meaningful.**

Activity 25

Test Hackman and Oldham's ideas against your own experience. Try to think of someone you know who is highly motivated; does he or she:

■ get good feedback – directly or indirectly? | YES | NO |

■ have a high level of control over the work? | YES | NO |

■ have the chance to apply a range of skills and abilities? | YES | NO |

■ complete clearly identifiable tasks? | YES | NO |

■ have a good knowledge of the significance of these tasks? | YES | NO |

Now try to think of someone who does not appear to you to be well motivated, and answer the same questions about this person. Does he or she:

■ get good feedback – directly or indirectly? | YES | NO |

■ have a high level of control over the work? | YES | NO |

■ have the chance to apply a range of skills and abilities? | YES | NO |

■ complete clearly identifiable tasks? | YES | NO |

■ have a good knowledge of the significance of these tasks? | YES | NO |

It seems to be a common experience that when all these job characteristics are present, then motivation is high, and stays high.

Perhaps you have observed someone who seems to be well motivated, and yet you believe that some of the core characteristics of the job, listed above, are not exhibited. This most often happens when someone first takes on a job; however, almost inevitably, motivation will fall off after a while. A new recruit to a company will typically be keen to do a good job, but become disillusioned if feedback is poor, or there is little autonomy, or the job-holder does not experience meaningfulness.

We'll take up these ideas again in Session C. Meanwhile, try the Self-assessment.

Self-assessment 2

1   Complete the diagram below by filling in with words from this list:

FOOD   STABILITY   AFFECTION
FRIENDSHIP   ACHIEVEMENT   SELF-RESPECT
PERSONAL DEVELOPMENT   ACCEPTANCE   WATER

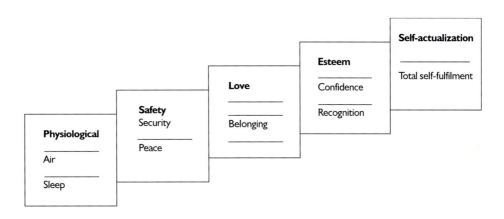

2   McGregor's Theory X and Theory Y are two sets of assumptions about working people.

Which of the following statements reflect a Theory X perception of employees, and which a Theory Y? Write 'X' or 'Y' in the space provided.

Theory

a   People dislike work and will avoid it whenever possible.   _____

b   People, given the chance, will often exercise their own
    self-direction and self-control at work.   _____

c   The average person seeks responsibility at work.   _____

d Most working people have relatively limited ambitions and prefer to be told what to do. _____

e The best way to motivate people is to provide them with wages and job security. _____

f The expenditure of physical and mental effort is as natural as play or rest. _____

3 In Herzberg's two-factor theory, which of the following should be classed as motivators and which should be classed as maintenance factors? Write 'Motivator' or 'Maintenance' in the space provided:

a Acknowledgement for a job well done. _____

b Job security. _____

c The chance for promotion. _____

d The opportunity to gain new knowledge. _____

e Working conditions. _____

f The job itself. _____

4 Fill in the blanks in the following sentences:

Performance   depends upon   _____

_____   depends upon   Reward

Effort   depends upon   _____

_____   depends upon   Performance

5 In the following table, put a tick in the correct column on the right against each essential job characteristic:

	What the worker gets from each job characteristic:		
The essential job characteristics:	Knowledge of the actual results of the work activities	Experienced responsibility for outcomes of the work	Experienced meaningfulness of the work
Autonomy			
Skill variety			
Task significance			
Task identity			
Feedback from job			

Answers to these questions can be found on page 81.

7 Summary

- Maslow's hierarchy of needs suggests that there are five sets of goals or basic needs. Only when one need is fulfilled does the next 'higher' need occupy the mind.

- McGregor's Theory X is the set of assumptions that people dislike work and need to be controlled and directed.

- McGregor's Theory Y is the idea that people will, under the right conditions, enjoy work, seek responsibility and control themselves.

- Herzberg's two-factor theory indicates that the factors causing job satisfaction are not the direct opposite of those causing dissatisfaction. Satisfaction can be found in the work itself: achievement; recognition; work itself; responsibility; advancement. The sources of dissatisfaction are in the work environment: working conditions, company policy and administration; supervision; interpersonal relations; salary; status; job security.

- Expectancy theory refers to the expectations of an employee and the cycle of cause and effect between motivation, effort, performance and reward.

- Hackman and Oldham's ideas suggest that there are certain essential job characteristics (feedback; autonomy; skill variety; task identity; task significance) which are all necessary if a worker is to be motivated to work well.

Session C Making work more rewarding

1 Introduction

Having covered a good deal of theory, we can now come to the question of how to go about the business of motivating staff.

Following on from what we have discussed, particularly the Hackman and Oldham proposals, we will look at how greater efficiency can be achieved by designing work.

First though, we look at a well-established system which adopts quite a different approach.

2 Taking the skill out of work

Organizations have always been interested in efficiency and increased productivity. However, they have not always taken the approach of achieving it by trying to increase staff motivation.

One system which has been widely used is based on what is called the **micro-division of labour**. This system was – and in some cases, still is – employed in factories running automated assembly lines.

The principle behind the micro-division of labour is that jobs are broken down into the smallest possible elements. A high level of automation is used, so the workers perform very simple tasks. This means for one thing that almost anyone can very quickly learn to do any particular job with the minimum of training.

41

Activity 26

3 mins

From the point of view of factory efficiency, can you think of some other advantages of this system? Suggest **two** advantages if you can.

_____

_____

_____

_____

Some other advantages are that:

■ production does not depend on skilled people and so the absence of any individual does not interfere with the work; in fact, absenteeism is much less of a problem than it is with other systems, because new people can be quickly trained to 'fill in';

■ the work is not demanding and so long shifts can be worked – at least, that is the theory;

■ the work can be very closely controlled; for instance, if it is found that a certain operation is being done incorrectly it can be quickly traced to a single operator.

So much for the advantages. There is certainly no doubt that factories using this system have been very effective at producing large quantities of goods cheaply.

But there is another side to the story.

There are a number of disadvantages of this system. If we look at it from the production worker's point of view:

■ jobs are monotonous and boring;

■ unlike machines, people are not very good at doing repetitive work: they lose concentration because they have nothing to keep their interest;

■ there's no scope to do the work better or more quickly: machines control the rate of work;

■ people who work on assembly lines have little opportunity for social contact.

Activity 27

3 mins

What might be the negative effects of these disadvantages on efficiency? Write down **two** possible effects.

_____

_____

_____

_____

Some of the effects are that:

- when jobs are boring, people tend to make mistakes;
- people who lose concentration are more liable to have accidents;
- where the work is demeaning and there is no scope for personal development, workers may actually become antagonistic towards their employer; this can lead to wildcat strikes and even sabotage (literally putting spanners in the works!);
- there is likely to be a high rate of turnover.

All these things will either reduce output or increase costs – or both.

For these reasons and others organizations are turning against this system. Instead they have looked for ways of motivating people to take an interest in and responsibility for their work.

3 Reviewing the theory

At this point we can start to tie some of the theory together.

Let's recap:

- **Maslow's hierarchy of needs**

Maslow showed that people are only preoccupied with basic survival and safety when these things are under threat. Otherwise, they tend to 'climb' to greater goals and needs, including a sense of belonging, self-respect and self-fulfilment.

- **Theory X and Theory Y**

McGregor proposed that, rather than disliking work and responsibility, people will, under the right conditions, enjoy work and seek responsibility. They prefer to control and direct themselves, rather than being regulated from above.

A fairly recent concept in management is that of **empowerment,** which, in broad terms, means managers stepping back and giving individuals and workteams the power to organize their own work. Empowerment could be said to be a realization of McGregor's ideas under Theory Y.

■ **Herzberg's two factor theory**

Herzberg's work indicates that the factors causing job satisfaction are not the same as those causing dissatisfaction. The motivators – such as recognition, responsibility and job interest – can be found in an employee's relationship to what he or she does. The maintenance factors – such as working conditions, salary and status – are more to do with the work environment.

■ **Expectancy theory**

This refers to the expectations of an employee and the cycle of cause and effect between motivation, effort, performance and reward. If the reward does not provide the motivation, the motivation does not lead to effort, the effort does not result in the required performance, then the reward will not be earned.

■ **Hackman and Oldham**

This theory is best summed up in the table we looked at:

The essential job characteristics:	What the worker gets from them:	The result, if all these job characteristics are present:
Feedback from job	→ Knowledge of the actual results of the work activities	
Autonomy	→ Experienced responsibility for outcomes of the work	High internal work motivation
Skill variety Task identity Task significance	→ Experienced meaningfulness of the work	

Then we considered the advantages and disadvantages of the micro-division of labour. We saw that when people are treated as if they were machines they performed badly and reacted against the system and the organization.

Activity 28

2 mins

Which one of the theories above do you think reflects the development of the system of taking away responsibility and breaking down jobs into small easily-controlled tasks?

Micro-division of labour seems to be backed up by McGregor's Theory X – the view of management that workers want to be controlled and that they dislike responsibility.

The main problem with the micro-division of labour is that the jobs are designed as if people were robots, and not very clever robots at that. Many organizations have now moved completely away from this idea, and have redesigned their workplaces to be more efficient by **enriching** jobs, rather than simplifying them.

4 Job enrichment

There is now a trend towards **job enrichment** (although this particular term may not be used by all organizations). Job enrichment means designing work and workplaces so that people have:

- more responsibility;
- more scope for self-development;
- more control over the work they do;
- more feedback on results.

Activity 29

Which of the theories above tend to support the trend towards job enrichment?

_____

_____

I would say that those of McGregor, Maslow, Herzberg, and Hackman and Oldham all do.

- McGregor's Theory Y put up the idea that people like work and responsibility.
- Maslow suggested that people have greater needs than simply survival and security.
- Herzberg showed that job interest, achievement, recognition, responsibility and advancement were the main motivators.
- Hackman and Oldham suggested that feedback, responsibility and meaningfulness are all requirements for motivation.

But before we continue any further on this theme, let us clarify what job enrichment **is** and what it **is not**.

5 Job rotation and job enlargement

'The utility man typically has no more self-control, only slightly more knowledge of results and only a slightly greater chance to test his valued abilities.' — Edward E. Lawler, (1969) *Job Design and Employee Motivation*.

Job enrichment should not be confused with two other approaches to job redesign: job rotation and job enlargement.

Job rotation involves switching people between a number of different jobs of relatively similar complexity. An example of this would be to allow production workers to swap from one part of the assembly line to another.

Although job rotation has the advantage of increasing flexibility, **it does not increase motivation**. A young bank employee summed it up when she said:

'After I'd been at the bank a few months I became bored with my job. They introduced job rotation and now I move from one boring job to another!'

Job enlargement involves adding more tasks of similar complexity to the job. Once again, **motivation is not improved**. Applied to our bank clerk, she might well have said:

'After I'd been at the bank a few months I became bored with my job. They introduced job enlargement and now I have several more boring tasks added to the job!'

Activity 30

3 mins

Bearing in mind the theory we've covered, what reason can you give for job rotation and job enlargement failing to motivate?

_____

_____

_____

EXTENSION 4
Charles B. Handy discusses job design and job enlargement in his book *Understanding Organisations*.

I hope you agree that job rotation and job enlargement both fail to motivate because they do not offer the opportunity for growth. Doing more things or different things of the same complexity does not allow people to build on experience and knowledge.

Job enrichment, on the other hand, does just that. We can first look at it in terms of the Hackman and Oldham theory. It generally involves:

- adding **skill variety**, by increasing the number of complex tasks to a job over a period of time. Such tasks are designed to give people the chance to develop underused skills and abilities.

- providing increased **task significance**: designing the work to be important, so that others depend on its outcome. (Organizations are encouraging staff to see others as customers of their work, these days, which fits in well with the idea of increased task significance.)
- presenting new tasks as **opportunities** rather than demands. This offers a degree of choice as to what tasks to do and when to do them. More complex tasks can be taken on as and when they feel able to cope.
- giving people and teams greater **autonomy**: allowing more discretion in the way that the job is paced, checked, sequenced and so on. You may hear the word **empowerment**, which, as mentioned earlier, means managers stepping back and giving workteams the power to run themselves.
- setting up systems that ensure fast, direct **feedback**.

When designing for job enrichment, Maslow's work must also be borne in mind: people won't be ready to satisfy these 'higher' needs if more basic wants have not been satisfied.

And our reading of Herzberg should remind us that maintenance or hygiene factors may get in the way of motivation.

What about expectancy theory? That tells us that staff should be able to see that:

- there is a link between effort and performance, and between performance and reward;
- the distribution of rewards is fair;
- rewards are worth having, in their own eyes.

6 Job enrichment in practice

Let us look at two very different examples of job enrichment in practice.

6.1 The case of Motorola

Paul Noakes, Motorola's Director of External Quality Programmes, feels they have learned something about motivation. He has said:

'I give lots of quality presentations around the world and my message is that our role as managers today is to get out of people's way. We have got to give them the resources, the tools and to see that they are properly trained. As old-style managers we created many problems. People say: 'How do you get your people motivated?' and I reply: 'We've never had a people problem. What we really had was a management problem.' When I used to run factories, people would say: 'Give me some smart people and I'll show you what I can do. All I have is bunch of dummies!' Back then, we always spoke about our people being the problem. But really we were the problem!'

One new style of job design adopted by Motorola is called **self-managed team working**, or 'self-directed work teams', as Motorola refer to the idea.

'We got into self-directed work teams (SDWTs) six or seven years ago. It started slowly and in a couple of the facilities. One facility outside Buffalo, New York, is called Elmer New York: their production operation consists totally of SDWTs. They have no supervision. They have a production manager and the teams are organized there. They will be teams of typically about fifteen or twenty people. These teams set their own objectives.

We have a corporate quality goal, a cycle-time goal and everything else that drives it, and a customer satisfaction criterion which that says that we cannot let anything happen to disturb the customer.

The teams do their own interviewing for their members. They have asked for the right to terminate, which we have not given them, because we have a company policy, whereby if you have ten or more years of service, you can't be terminated for any reason without the Chairman's approval. We also operate in a non-union environment around the world. Those things we are very careful about.

The teams also decide how to divide up their work. They are mostly trained in more than one job. If they want to trade off, that is their business. They elect their own team-leader who in a sense is a supervisor. Their team-leader reports on what they are doing and so forth. There is great satisfaction from this: people really do enjoy their work.'

The idea of allowing teams to manage themselves is not a new one, but it is only quite recently that large organizations have dared to try it out in this kind of way.

There are many risks to this policy, and there is no doubt that **what managers generally fear most is losing control**. If people are allowed to organize themselves, they say, there will be anarchy: productivity and quality will fall, accidents will rise, and the customer will be alienated. So far, for Motorola, things haven't worked out that way.

You may or may not applaud Motorola's approach, but it is being adopted by others, and may be the pattern for future work design. A recent survey (July 1995) by the Industrial Society, of more than 500 personnel professionals in the UK, found that more than one in three are already reporting the adoption of self-managed teams. Double that proportion were expecting this method of working to be widespread in two to three years.

6.2 Enriched jobs in voluntary work

Rani Akinyemi and Betty Dunphy are volunteers working in a centre caring for mentally handicapped children. During the course of a typical week, they get:

Skill variety. They're expected to carry out a variety of tasks around the centre, which exercise their skills in a number of ways, including:

- manual work;
- planning skills (e.g., for outings);
- communicating skills;
- calculating skills (Betty often helps out with the accounts);
- caring skills;
- cooking skills.

Task identity. For the most part, they are expected to complete whole tasks.

Task significance. They are aware that the children and others depend on them, sometimes critically.

Autonomy. There aren't enough people for there to be much close supervision, so Rani and Betty are relied upon to organize their work as they see fit.

Feedback from the job. The most rewarding feedback is to see the children respond to them, and show real affection.

Needless to say, Rani and Betty are highly motivated!

Before you go on to the next session, which is about the team leader's role, try the Self-assessment questions.

Self-assessment 3

Fill in the blanks in the sentences on the left with the correct phrases taken from the list in capitals below.

AUTONOMY, COMPLEXITY, FEEDBACK FROM THE JOB,
JOB ROTATION, JOB ENLARGEMENT, MICRO-DIVISION OF LABOUR,
SKILL VARIETY, SMALLEST, TASKS, TASK IDENTITY,
TASK SIGNIFICANCE

1 The principle behind the _____ is that jobs are broken down into the _____ possible elements.

2 Job enrichment means designing jobs so that people have more _____ , _____ , _____ , _____ , and _____ .

3 _____ involves switching people between a number of different jobs of relatively similar _____ .

4 _____ involves adding more _____ of similar complexity to the job.

For questions 5 to 8, decide whether each statement is TRUE, FALSE or SOMETIMES TRUE.

5 When jobs are broken down into very simple tasks that anyone can learn, the problem of staff turnover becomes unimportant: you 'just recruit more people off the street'. TRUE/FALSE/SOMETIMES TRUE

6 Job enrichment is very hard to implement, because it entails lots of training to do more complex tasks. TRUE/FALSE/SOMETIMES TRUE

7 Job enrichment programmes should be presented as opportunities, not demands. TRUE/FALSE/SOMETIMES TRUE

8 Small organizations can't implement job enrichment programmes, as they have not the resources of large companies. TRUE/FALSE/SOMETIMES TRUE

9 Which of the following ideas support the concept of job enrichment?

 a Herzberg's theory that job interest is a motivator.
 b Maslow's theory that people who are starving have no interest in self-development.
 c McGregor's Theory X: that people dislike work and responsibility.
 d McGregor's Theory Y: that people prefer to control themselves than be controlled from above.
 e Hackman and Oldham's theories about the prerequisites for internal motivation.

The answers to these questions can be found on page 83.

7 Summary

- The micro-division of labour is the breaking down of jobs into their simplest possible elements. It is ultimately inefficient.

- Job rotation is the switching of people between jobs of similar complexity.

- Job enlargement involves adding more tasks of similar complexity to a job.

- Job enrichment means designing jobs so that people have:

  - skill variety;
  - task identity;
  - task significance;
  - autonomy;
  - feedback from the job.

Session D The team leader's role

1 Introduction

Team leaders have a vital role in motivating people. It might almost be said that this is their main function, for a team that is not motivated will invariably perform badly. The team leader is, among other things:

- a coach, who aims to bring out the best in people;
- a facilitator, who clears away obstacles to enable the team to make unimpeded progress;
- an empowering agent, providing the team with the skills and information to manage themselves.

Whatever your title, you are a team leader if you run a team.

In this part of the workbook we are going to discuss how the ideas of motivation we've covered can be applied by team leaders.

2 Needs and your team

You may recall that Abraham Maslow identified five levels of human needs or goals:

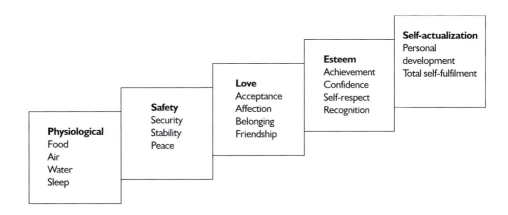

Let's refresh our memories on the ways in which rewards of work can help to satisfy each of these needs.

53

Activity 31

8 mins

List up to **two** things which can be provided by an organization (such as yours) for its employees or volunteers, in order to help satisfy **each** level of Maslow's needs. I have included an example of each in the list below.

Physiological

- canteen facilities
- _____
- _____

Safety

- safe working conditions
- _____
- _____

Love

- the chance to work in a group
- _____
- _____

Esteem

- praise for work done
- _____
- _____

Self-actualization

- interesting work
- _____
- _____

Answers to these questions can be found on page 85.

Team leaders can't always control the provision of all these things, although they may be able to have a strong influence.

Let's now go on to look at some of the ways in which team leaders can play a direct part in motivating members of their teams.

3 Motivation and the team

Whether you are an appointed team leader, or were elected as leader of a self-managed team, you have to try to ensure that each person in your workteam is able to perform at work in the best way possible. This probably involves a series of complex tasks, which may include:

■ planning work in advance;
■ organizing things so that materials and equipment are available when and where they're needed;
■ making sure team members are properly trained;
■ providing clear information about what is required;
■ giving feedback on results.

As we have been discussing, perhaps more than anything else it involves helping them to find the motivation to do the job well.

We have talked about job enrichment, but it is important to remember that different things motivate different people: there is no straightforward answer to the question:

'How do I motivate my team members?'

Activity 32

How can you find out what motivates each member of your workteam? Make **one** suggestion.

_____

_____

_____

You might have suggested simply asking them. This is one approach. But will they be able to tell you? Our dictionary definition of motivation was 'A conscious or unconscious driving force. . . .': people aren't always aware of what motivates them.

A more realistic suggestion is to

get to know the members of your team

in order to get an understanding of what they want and expect from work. Of course, this statement is very easily made, but may not be so easy to put into practice.

Activity 33

3 mins

Can you write down **one** reason why a team leader may find it hard to get to know team members well?

_____

_____

_____

For one thing, there is often a perceived status gap between a team leader and the rest of the team, which may get in the way of a true and complete understanding of attitudes and values.

Another thing that gets in the way of knowing people is that many people hide their real feelings.

A further difficulty is that the needs and attitudes of people aren't necessarily fixed. It is dangerous to assume that someone will react the same way to a set of circumstances in the future to the way she or he has reacted in the past.

Nevertheless, if you want to be able to provide the motivation the team members want, there's no effective alternative to talking with them, working with them and observing them in action.

3.1 What the team leader can do

Returning to the question of what you can do, as a team leader, to motivate your team members, let's summarize the areas where you might have the opportunity to take some actions.

■ **Engender the right kind of climate or atmosphere.**

The atmosphere of an organization is determined by the policies of management and by the attitudes of everyone working there. Local team leaders do have some control over atmosphere within the group or section where they operate. If you are willing to adopt an open, sharing approach to your team and your work, there's a good chance others will do the same. Don't expect overnight miracles, however!

■ **Give rewards where they're deserved.**

Activity 34

Think for a few minutes of what rewards you can offer your team. Remember that motivation is derived from the expectation of a reward, but that rewards do not have to be tangible ones.

Try to suggest **three** rewards that you might offer.

_____

_____

_____

Any team leader can reward the members of his or her team by:

- being generous in **praise** of their achievements;
- giving **thanks** for efforts made and personal contributions made;
- giving feedback in the form of **constructive criticism** – a point we'll expand upon shortly;
- recognizing the needs of the **individual**, and the part played by each person in the collective effort, rather than treating people as if they were all the same;
- trying to improve **social** relationships, by, for example, setting out work areas so that it is easy for team members to communicate;
- giving **recognition** of extra effort;
- giving **responsibility** where it is deserved and wanted.

Many other rewards may be in your power to bestow. They may range from buying a team member a drink to putting up someone's name for promotion.

■ **Promote the intrinsic worth of the job.**

We have seen that 'task significance' is an essential ingredient for high motivation. One of your functions, as team leader, is to 'sell' to the team the inherent value of the job they are doing, and point out the ways in which the outcome affects others.

■ **Keep the workteam informed.**

Your team members will want to feel fully involved in the organization they work for, and will take a professional interest in events and reports concerning the kind of work they do. You can play a part in keeping them abreast of developments.

■ **Be fair in allocating work.**

One thing that can get in the way of motivation is a perceived unfairness in task allocation: 'She gets all the easy jobs. I have to struggle through with the horrible ones.'

57

There's nothing surprising in this kind of reaction. We have already discussed the fact that status is a maintenance factor; perceived inequities in work assignment are often interpreted as a difference in the position of one person compared with another.

■ **Make work fun.**

You may not agree with this suggestion. Work is important to most people, and may be taken very seriously. But it doesn't mean you can't be light-hearted, enjoy a joke, and see the humorous side of things. If you can manage to make work fun, you will have gone a long way to motivating your team.

■ **Take account of the circumstances under which people have to work.**

Few of us are lucky enough to work in an ideal environment, where all the resources we need are available to us. You, as a leader, may be unable to provide the working conditions you would like to. Your team may include one or more of the following groups, for example: volunteers; short-term contract staff; part-time staff; temporary employees.

The motivation of an unpaid volunteer will be rather different from a permanent member of staff building a long-term career. The volunteer may be self-motivated to a large extent, but will nevertheless still need plenty of support and encouragement.

Temporary and part-time staff may not feel that they are part of the team at all, and are very often treated as though they have no need of motivation beyond their pay. If you can spend a little time in giving such staff background information, and show that you value their contribution, you may be surprised at how much better motivated they can be.

■ **Give your team members scope for development.**

For many workers, the main attraction of a job is the opportunities it offers for development and growth. This is particularly true of young people, and when the job is poorly paid (or not paid at all). You can:

■ look out for suitable openings for team members, within the job or in other parts of the organization;
■ give information and training which will enable people to develop their talents
■ encourage and help individuals to take available, and appropriate opportunities.

■ **Avoid threats to security.**

As Herzberg observed, job insecurity is a threat and a demotivating factor. We discussed already the fact that most people are not normally motivated by the fact of having a job, but may become very demotivated should there be a threat of losing it.

■ **Make the team's targets and objectives clear.**

Even teams with a high degree of autonomy need to be reminded what they are trying to achieve. Having a clear goal is a great motivator.

3.2 Motivation in an uncertain atmosphere

You may have been in the position of seeing:

■ the organization being 'rationalized' or down-sized;
■ colleagues being made redundant;
■ uncertainty about the economic future of the organization.

How do you keep up morale and motivation in these circumstances?

Some suggestions to add to your own ideas are:

■ seeking information, and passing on as clear a picture of the situation as you are able, because anxiety feeds on doubt, and rumours tend to abound when there's no clear message coming through;
■ countering cynicism with a positive approach that encourages people to make the best of things as they are, and to plan for the future;
■ keeping the team occupied with meaningful work – which, where others have been made redundant, there is probably no shortage of – but not letting them get overwhelmed;
■ in the case of those who have been left behind when friends and colleagues have been 'let go', acknowledging and discussing the guilt that is likely to be felt;
■ talking with people and establishing new, mutually supportive relationships;
■ treating one another with respect.

4 Job enrichment

The following activity will help you to focus on job enrichment in your workplace.

4.1 What do we mean by job enrichment?

How much influence and control you have when it comes to introducing job enrichment depends on the kind of work you do and the kind of organization you work for.

What is important is that you recognize the value of job enrichment and promote and encourage it whenever and wherever you can.

Activity 35

3 mins

The list below suggests some ways in which job enrichment might be introduced. Place a tick against each item which you think you might have the authority or influence to implement for your team.

a Letting the workteam members see a job through from start to finish. ☐

b Enhancing task significance. ☐

c Increasing levels of responsibility. ☐

d Reducing the level of supervision, giving the team members greater control over the work. ☐

e Providing more feedback over results. ☐

f Introducing greater skill variety, perhaps by increasing the range of tasks by delegation. ☐

g Giving an individual the opportunity to become expert in some specific task. ☐

4.2 Would it work?

Is job enrichment right for your team? Introducing a programme of job enrichment can be a big step. You will need to think about what you want to achieve and how best to achieve it.

Go through the following checklist to help you decide whether embarking on a job enrichment programme could be right for your team.

Activity 36

2 mins

Answer the following questions.

Question			Comment
■ Do you believe the jobs of your team members can be enriched?	YES	NO	In general, the answer must be YES. All evidence suggests that any job can be enriched.
■ Will they take up the opportunities offered by their enriched job?	YES	NO	That's your judgement. Not everyone is looking for job enrichment, but most people welcome it.
■ Will a job enrichment programme improve performance?	YES	NO	Experience shows that it usually does. Herzberg demonstrated in a number of studies that job enrichment achieves increased productivity.
■ Will management support you if you embark on a job enrichment programme?	YES	NO	Crucial question! An extensive programme should not be taken lightly.
■ Will training be required?	YES	NO	The changes you introduce may not be possible without an associated training programme. If you are restricted on the amount of training you can provide, this fact should be taken into account.

4.2 Which jobs?

What kind of jobs would lend themselves to job enrichment?

Look at jobs where:

- job satisfaction is low;
- maintenance factors are costly;
- changes would not be expensive;
- lack of motivation is affecting performance.

Activity 37

10 mins

List the jobs done by your team which meet some or all of these criteria.

■ Jobs where job satisfaction is low are:

_____

_____

_____

_____

■ Jobs where maintenance factors are costly are:

_____

_____

_____

_____

■ Jobs where changes would not be expensive are:

_____

_____

_____

_____

■ Jobs where lack of motivation is affecting performance are:

_____

_____

_____

_____

Select the jobs that appear on at least two of these lists. They may be the best ones where job enrichment can be implemented.

_____

_____

_____

_____

4.3 How can you devise appropriate changes?

One technique is to try 'brainstorming' – listing as many changes as you can that may enrich the job **even if they seem impossible to apply**. Brainstorming is usually thought of as a group activity, but it can be almost as useful to work on your own. Take a blank sheet of paper and write down all the possible ways you can think of to enrich the jobs of your team. Then, when you've run out of ideas, eliminate:

- those changes that involve maintenance factors, rather than motivation factors;
- those changes which, for some clear reason, are not practical;
- those changes which appear to be job enlargement, rather than job enrichment.

4.4 How should the changes be presented?

Present them as **opportunities**!

4.5 How can you decide whether the changes are effective?

You should find ways of **measuring** the result of the changes. One approach is to set up a 'controlled experiment' in order to measure the success or otherwise of job enrichment programmes. You may feel you do not have time for such a trial. Nevertheless, it is vital that you establish some way of measuring the change in performance.

Portfolio of evidence C9.4

Activity 38

5 mins

This Activity will provide you with a basis for a structured approach to the assessment of development activities. If you develop your responses into a detailed plan, it would form useful evidence for your S/NVQ portfolio. If you are intending to take this course of action, it might be better to write your answers on separate sheets of paper.

Some ways of measuring are listed below. Tick those that you think would be appropriate to you.

- by volume of production ☐
- by number of sales made ☐
- by number of customer complaints ☐
- by value of work produced ☐
- by quality of work produced ☐
- by value of sales ☐
- by amount of wastage or scrap ☐
- by bonus earned ☐
- by amount of rework ☐
- by cost per unit produced ☐
- by reduction in absenteeism ☐
- by reduction in lateness ☐
- by reduction in lost time through accidents ☐

My ideas for measuring changes would be

_____

_____

_____

_____

_____

4.6 How soon can you expect to see results?

When introducing job enrichment, be prepared for some initial drop in performance – don't forget that people may take a while to get used to the new ideas. However, this effect should not last for long and you should not let it deter you.

5 Job enrichment and the team

There are things that can be done to introduce job enrichment, which team leaders have the power to implement. They include:

- delegating tasks and responsibilities, so that team members have more control over their work;
- giving communications and feedback;
- modifying the level of supervision given, to increase autonomy.

Let us examine each of these more closely.

5.1 Delegating

Along with other team leaders, you are able to exercise some control over the work of your team.

You also have the choice of doing all of your own work yourself or allowing your workteam to take on some of it.

In other words, you can **delegate** some of your own work and/or your responsibilities.

You may find the following procedure helpful in the process of delegation.

a Make a list of tasks and responsibilities which you normally do yourself, which might possibly be delegated. Don't forget to include those jobs you never quite get around to doing!

b Make sure you haven't included those jobs which you can't delegate – such as responsibility for safety.

c Consider allocating the tasks to specific team members, by answering the questions:

'Is this task within the capability of this individual? If so, would he or she find it challenging and rewarding?'

d Allocate the task, making clear what is to be achieved. Provide training where necessary.

e Follow up by checking that people aren't in difficulties and that progress is being made.

f Do not use delegation as an excuse to get rid of jobs you dislike doing. Never delegate anything you are not prepared to do yourself.

Like all job enrichment, delegated tasks are an opportunity; they shouldn't be made into demands.

Remember too that:

you can't avoid the responsibility for a task by getting others to do it for you.

65

5.2 Giving feedback

As we discussed in Sessions B and C, direct feedback from the job is generally preferable to reported feedback. Nevertheless, many teams are unable to get sufficient feedback from the job itself, and rely on the team leader to keep them informed of progress. Even when there is plenty of direct feedback, people need it reinforced from time to time. They want to know that you are satisfied with the results they are achieving.

Activity 39

2 mins

How often do you let individual team members know how well they are doing?

Most of the time. ☐
On the odd occasion. ☐

How often do you feed back information about the effects the team's work has had, by (say) telling them how well received it was by a customer or another department?

Most of the time. ☐
On the odd occasion. ☐

If you don't tell them often enough, how will they get to know? Everybody needs to know how well they are achieving objectives, and what the results of their work are. They need to be able to see, too, that the outcome of their work is having a significant effect on the lives of others.

5.3 Constructive criticism

We have talked about feedback, but if you are to let your team know how well they are doing, it usually isn't sufficient to say something like: 'Everything seems OK – keep it up.'

People need to know **how** well they are doing, not simply **whether** they are doing well. Even the most sensitive person will respond to criticism in a positive way, if it is given in an appropriate manner and spirit. Preferably the feedback should come immediately the results of the work are known.

Let's take an example. A professional singer who performs publicly will get a certain amount of feedback from the audience. If there is rapturous applause at the end of a performance, the singer will be pleased with herself, because she will know that she has sung well. Even then, however, the singer may be conscious of certain flaws in her performance, and worried whether there were any others she has not noticed. She will probably want to find ways to improve her delivery: the next audience may not be so easily pleased!

For these reasons, the singer may look to others for constructive criticism: her music teacher, the producer of the concert or show, colleagues, professional critics and friends. She may also spend hours listening to recordings of her own voice. The singer, like anyone else desiring to improve their performance, is very interested in getting detailed feedback about the results of her work.

It goes without saying that all criticism should be given with tact and diplomacy, and the critic must be careful not to trigger any negative reactions.

> One of the characters in *Of Human Bondage*, by W. Somerset Maugham, said: 'People ask you for criticism, but they only want praise.'
>
> Is this your experience?

Portfolio of evidence C12.3

Activity 40

8 mins

If you develop your responses into a detailed plan, it would form useful evidence for your S/NVQ portfolio. If you are intending to take this course of action, it might be better to write your answers on separate sheets of paper.

Write down answers to the following questions. What changes do you intend to make:

■ to the frequency or timing of feedback you give to your team?

_____

_____

_____

■ in the method you use to give feedback to your team members, i.e., the way that you convey the messages?

_____

_____

_____

■ in the content of the feedback messages you give to your team?

_____

_____

_____

5.4 Giving your team members more scope

Increasing autonomy is a significant step towards job enrichment.

Portfolio of evidence C9.1

Activity 41

15 mins

You could develop this Activity to cover each member of your team. This will give you a plan for giving your team greater autonomy and control, thereby encouraging and stimulating them to make the best use of their abilities. If you develop your responses into a detailed plan, it would form useful evidence for your S/NVQ portfolio. If you are intending to take this course of action, it might be better to write your answers on separate sheets of paper.

To what extent is your workteam controlled? Take a few minutes and think about the work done by one member of your team. Then tick the appropriate boxes. Next, for each of the NOT AT ALL answers, say what actions you intend to take to give the team member greater control.

Job title _____

To what extent can he or she:	NOT AT ALL	TO SOME DEGREE	A GOOD DEAL
■ control the pace of the work?	☐	☐	☐

Proposed actions _____

_____

	NOT AT ALL	TO SOME DEGREE	A GOOD DEAL
■ determine the order or sequence in which the work is done?	☐	☐	☐

Proposed actions _____

_____

	NOT AT ALL	TO SOME DEGREE	A GOOD DEAL
■ decide how the work is done	☐	☐	☐

Proposed actions _____

_____

	NOT AT ALL	TO SOME DEGREE	A GOOD DEAL
■ decide when the work is done?	☐	☐	☐

Proposed actions _____

_____

	NOT AT ALL	TO SOME DEGREE	A GOOD DEAL
■ choose the tools, equipment or materials used for the job?	☐	☐	☐

Proposed actions _____

_____

	NOT AT ALL	TO SOME DEGREE	A GOOD DEAL
■ influence the quality of work produced?	☐	☐	☐

Proposed actions _____

_____

	NOT AT ALL	TO SOME DEGREE	A GOOD DEAL
■ decide where the work is done?	☐	☐	☐

Proposed actions _____

_____

By giving the team the opportunity for greater autonomy, you may feel you will lose control completely! The key is in careful planning: you need to be sure that the changes will work, and you must be ready to support team members when they need you. You cannot afford to sacrifice achievement of the team's objectives, simply in order to increase motivation; if you do, it is likely to have the opposite effect. The question that you have to answer is: 'How do I enrich the jobs of my team, and thereby increase their efficiency and effectiveness?'

Self-assessment 4

1 What advice would you give to a colleague at the same level as you who wanted to motivate his team? Say whether you think each of the following would be good or bad advice, and then explain your reasoning.

a 'Get to know your team members well.' **GOOD/BAD**

_____

_____

b 'Try to improve their working conditions.' **GOOD/BAD**

_____

_____

c 'Give them more scope and more involvement.' **GOOD/BAD**

_____

_____

d 'Watch them more closely, so they know you care about them.'
GOOD/BAD

_____

_____

2 Which of the following are dangers involved in delegation, and why?

a That jobs will be delegated for things which the team leader must retain personal responsibility for – such as safety. ☐

b That jobs will be delegated which everyone finds boring and unrewarding. ☐

c That team members will not carry out the jobs correctly. ☐

d That a team member will find the new job so rewarding that he or she will lose interest in other work. ☐

3   List three ways in which a team member might be given more control over the work she or he does.

_____

_____

_____

Answers to these questions can be found on page 83.

7 Summary

■   To know what motivates team members, you have to get to know them.

■   Organizations can provide the means to help satisfy all levels of needs of employees.

■   The team leader can implement the ideas of motivation and job enrichment by

- helping to engender the right climate;
- providing appropriate rewards;
- enriching jobs.

■   Job enrichment can entail

- delegating tasks;
- providing feedback;
- giving team members more scope.

Performance checks

1 Quick quiz

Jot down the answers to the following questions on *Motivating People*.

Question 1 Define the word 'motivation' in your own words.

_____

_____

Question 2 According to Maslow, there are five basic needs or goals. Esteem and self-actualization are two of them. What are the others, and in which order do they go?

_____

_____

Question 3 Theory X is a set of assumptions which McGregor thought many managers had about their employees. What approach does it suggest for getting people to do work?

_____

_____

Question 4 Theory Y is a more enlightened view than Theory X. What does it say about whether people like work or not?

_____

_____

Question 5 Looking now at Herzberg's ideas, what (briefly) is a 'maintenance factor'?

_____

_____

Question 6 According to expectancy theory, effort, reward, motivation and performance form a cycle of cause and effect. How do they relate: Performance depends on _____ ? Effort depends on _____?

Question 7 Name one possible cause of a breakdown between reward and motivation.

_____

_____

Question 8   From the organization's point of view, name two disadvantages of breaking jobs down into their simplest possible elements, so that they need little skill or training.

_____

_____

Question 9   According to Hackman and Oldham, which five job characteristics are essential for high internal work motivation?

_____

_____

Question 10   What is meant by job enlargement? Give a brief description in your own words.

_____

_____

Question 11   Now define job rotation, briefly.

_____

_____

Question 12   Which kind of jobs lend themselves most readily to job enrichment?

_____

_____

Question 13   When giving feedback about performance, (a) how soon should it be given; (b) what kind of feedback is best?

_____

_____

Question 14   We have used the term 'autonomy', without defining it. How would you explain what it means?

_____

_____

Question 15   Make three suggestions to someone who asks: 'How can I motivate my staff?'

_____

_____

Answers to these questions can be found on page 85.

2 Workbook assessment

Read the following case incident, and then deal with the questions which follow. Write your answers on a separate sheet of paper.

■ Nicole Petty worked at the head office of a travel company for ten years. Initially she found the work exciting and demanding but the pressures of work were very high. She was earning a good salary by the travel industry standards, but was becoming increasingly frustrated with the heavy work load.

When asked to manage a new travel agency office in Torquay, Nicole jumped at the chance, seeing this as an opportunity to spend less time on administration and more on 'being a travel agent'.

Nicole engaged three members of staff – two counter clerks, Jenny Downs and Darryl Proven, and a typist, Shanin Ahmed.

Nicole decided that she would organize the agency on a specialist basis as far as possible. All clients requiring an individual holiday would be referred to her and Nicole would design a package especially for them. This was the most difficult and interesting part of the work. However, she decided to let Jenny take care of the administrative side of these holidays. Nicole also decided to handle all business travel enquiries personally.

Darryl was to specialize in package holidays, while Jenny was to look after air, rail, coach and ferry reservations and ticketing, together with car hire and independent hotel bookings. Issues related to passports, visas, foreign currency, traveller's cheques and travel insurance were dealt with by both counter clerks.

The counter staff were obliged to enter all transactions in a central filing system for easy reference. Shanin was responsible for ensuring that information was correctly filed, although she spent most of her time on other clerical duties and typing correspondence dictated by Nicole and the two counter clerks. All letters were checked and signed by Nicole.

Prizes and incentives earned by the counter clerks for the sale of special offer package tours were pooled and redistributed equally between Jenny, Darryl and Shanin at the end of each month.

After three months of operation, Nicole reviewed the performance of the agency and was not pleased with what she found. Absenteeism was increasing and the timekeeping of the staff had deteriorated. A number of customers had complained about the 'off-hand manner' of the counter staff and about the quality of service in general. Some customers had even complained about the quality of the typed correspondence. Nicole approached her employees and expressed her concern. She was surprised to learn that all three were not happy with their wages and Darryl also added that he was bored with the job.

Nicole promised to review their wages and hinted that they would all receive a reasonable pay rise.

You only need to write **two** or **three** sentences in response to each question.

1 Using Herzberg's idea about money as a maintenance factor, describe the likely outcome of Nicole awarding her people a substantial pay rise.

2 How could Nicole go about introducing job enrichment in the travel agency?

3 What would be the likely effects of introducing job enrichment?

4 Describe the job changes Nicole might make to enrich the jobs of the two counter clerks.

5 Advise Nicole as to any other changes she could make that might improve motivation.

3 Work-based assignment

Portfolio of evidence C9.1, C9.2

The time guide for this assignment gives you an approximate idea of how long it is likely to take you to write up your findings. You will find you need to spend some additional time gathering information, talking to colleagues, and thinking about the assignment.

In this workbook we have discussed some ideas for enriching jobs. For this assignment, you should consider how job enrichment might be applied to the work of one member of your team.

This Assignment may provide the basis of appropriate evidence for your S/NVQ portfolio. It is designed to help you to demonstrate your ability to plan team development, by ensuring that your contributions to training and development plans:

- are consistent with team objectives and organizational values;
- reflect the identified training and development needs of all personnel for whom you have responsibility;
- are clear, relevant, realistic and take account of team and organizational constraints;
- are agreed with individual team members and take account of their work activities, learning ability and personal circumstances.

It will also help you to develop your Personal Competence in:

- building teams;
- relating to and showing sensitivity to others.

What you have to do

1 Select a job you feel would benefit from job enrichment.

2 Provide a brief description of the job as it now exists.

3 Describe, briefly, the changes you would like to see made to enrich the job. Explain how each change you've recommended would contribute to the process.

4 Then consider the expected effects of carrying out this plan – on the job, on the person concerned, on you and on the rest of the team.

75

Reflect and review

1 Reflect and review

Now that you have completed your work on *Motivating People*, let us review our workbook objectives.

■ You should be better able to identify some of the factors which tend to motivate and those which do not.

Our review of motivation theory should have given you plenty to think about. Herzberg's 'two factor theory' listed motivating factors (achievement; recognition; work itself; responsibility; advancement) and maintenance or hygiene factors (working conditions, company policy and administration; supervision; interpersonal relations; salary; status; job security). Hackman and Oldham suggested that certain core job characteristics (feedback from the job, autonomy, skill variety, task identity and task significance) are all essential for internal motivation.

Now you might like to consider how you could answer the following questions.

■ Which maintenance factors, through not being properly provided for, are tending to demotivate my team members?

_____

_____

■ Which motivation factors are missing or insufficiently provided for?

_____

_____

■ What plans am I going to make, in order to correct these deficiencies?

_____

_____

The second workbook objective was:

■ You should be better able to understand the behaviour of the people you work with.

As we have discussed, attaining a perfect understanding of other people is next to impossible. However, the better you know the members of your team, the more you will understand their behaviour and what makes them work well or

77

badly. Armed with the knowledge you have gained from this workbook, you should be better able to discover the motivation behind their behaviour.

■ What have I learned from this workbook that gives me greater insight into the behaviour of my team members? (Name at least one thing.)

_____

_____

■ What are my plans to get to know my team better?

_____

_____

The next workbook objective was:

■ You should be better able to put into effect the principles of job enrichment.

Job enrichment, as we interpreted it in the workbook, consists of giving individuals and teams greater autonomy, and setting up conditions so that there is: good feedback (preferably from the job itself); skill variety; task identity; task significance. Implementing a job enrichment programme is not usually easy, and requires thought and planning.

■ Which jobs, of which team members, do I intend to enrich?

_____

_____

■ How do I intend going about this, exactly?

_____

_____

The final objective was

■ You should be better able to find ways of motivating the members of your workteam.

This is the main purpose of the workbook. From your reading and understanding of the workbook, you are (we hope) better informed than you were. Your head is no doubt brimming with ideas about motivating the people who report to you. You may be sceptical of some of the theory and the ideas we've discussed, but you could do worse than try to apply them.

■ The following are the ideas which I intend to try out, in an effort to improve the motivation of my team members.

_____

_____

_____

2 Action plan

Use the plan on page 80 to further develop for yourself a course of action you want to take. Make a note in the left-hand column of the issues or problems you want to tackle, and then decide what you intend to do, and make a note in Column 2.

The resources you need might include time, materials, information or money. You may need to negotiate for some of them, but they could be something easily acquired, like half an hour of somebody's time, or a chapter of a book. Put whatever you need in Column 3. No plan means anything without a timescale, so put a realistic target completion date in Column 4.

Finally, describe the outcome you want to achieve as a result of this plan, whether it is for your own benefit or advancement, or a more efficient way of doing things.

3 Extensions

Extensions 1, 2 and 3

Book   *Management and Motivation*
Editors   V. H. Vroom and D. L. Deci
Edition   2nd edition, 1992
Publisher   Penguin Books

This is a 'classic' work and has recently been updated. It contains forty-two short pieces written by authorities in this field. It is the best book to buy if you want to review what the experts say about motivation.

Extension 4

Book   *Understanding Organisations*
Author   Charles B. Handy
Edition   4th edition, 1993
Publisher   Penguin Books

A general book on organizations, written by the famous Professor Handy, who has vast experience in the management field. The chapter called 'On the motivation to work' is the most relevant to our subject.

These Extensions can be taken up via your NEBS Management Centre. They will either have them or will arrange that you have access to them. However, it may be more convenient to check out the materials with your personnel or training people at work – they may well give you access. There are other good reasons for approaching your own people; for example, they will become aware of your interest and you can involve them in your development.

Desired outcomes

Actual outcomes

1 Issues

2 Action

3 Resources

4 Target completion

4 Answers to self-assessment questions

Self-assessment 1

1 To MOTIVATE somebody to do something, you have to get them to WANT to do it.

2 Managers need to be aware that VALUES and attitudes to work vary a great deal.

3 People aren't all motivated – or DEMOTIVATED – by the SAME things.

4 The ATMOSPHERE in the workplace is a KEY factor in motivating people.

5 You can motivate people by threatening them with violence. This is **false**: to motivate people, you have to get them to **want** to do something, not to **have** to do something.

6 You can motivate people by promising them rewards. This is **true**, as people will want to do the job to earn the reward.

7 Low absenteeism and high staff turnover are associated with a good atmosphere in an organization. This is **false**: low absenteeism and **low** staff turnover are associated with a good atmosphere in an organization.

8 An open, sharing atmosphere will tend to give people the scope to develop their skills and abilities. This is **true**: workers will feel involved and able to give of their best.

Self-assessment 2

1 The completed diagram is:

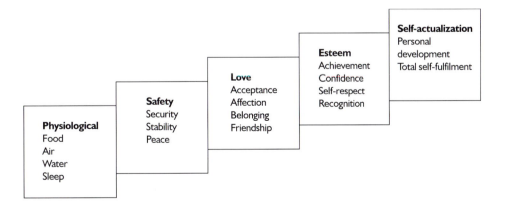

			Theory
2	a	People dislike work and will avoid it whenever possible.	X
	b	People, given the chance, will often exercise their own self-direction and self-control at work.	Y
	c	The average person seeks responsibility at work.	Y
	d	Most working people have relatively limited ambitions and prefer to be told what to do.	X
	e	The best way to motivate people is to provide them with wages and job security.	X
	f	The expenditure of physical and mental effort is as natural as play or rest.	Y

3	a	Acknowledgement for a job well done.	MOTIVATOR
	b	Job security.	MAINTENANCE
	c	The chance for promotion.	MOTIVATOR
	d	The opportunity to gain new knowledge.	MOTIVATOR
	e	Working conditions.	MAINTENANCE
	f	The job itself.	MOTIVATOR

4
Performance depends upon Effort
Motivation depends upon Reward
Effort depends upon Motivation
Reward depends upon Performance

5 The completed table is as follows:

	What the worker gets from each job characteristic:		
The essential job characteristics:	Knowledge of the actual results of the work activities	Experienced responsibility for outcomes of the work	Experienced meaningfulness of the work
Autonomy		✓	
Skill variety			✓
Task significance			✓
Task identity			✓
Feedback from job	✓		

Self-assessment 3 1. The principle behind the MICRO-DIVISION OF LABOUR is that jobs are broken down into the SMALLEST possible elements.

2 Job enrichment means designing jobs so that people have more SKILL VARIETY, TASK IDENTITY, AUTONOMY, TASK SIGNIFICANCE, and FEEDBACK FROM THE JOB. (In no particular order.)

3 JOB ROTATION involves switching people between a number of different jobs of relatively similar COMPLEXITY.

4 JOB ENLARGEMENT involves adding more TASKS of similar complexity to the job.

5 When jobs are broken down into very simple tasks that anyone can learn, the problem of staff turnover becomes unimportant: you 'just recruit more people off the street'. This is TRUE – if the organization is prepared to live with high levels of staff turnover.

6 Job enrichment is very hard to implement, because it entails lots of training to do more complex tasks. This is SOMETIMES TRUE: the amount of training required depends on the people doing the job. Often, job enrichment involves no training.

7 Job enrichment programmes should be presented as opportunities, not demands. This is TRUE.

8 Small organizations can't implement job enrichment programmes, as they do not have the resources of large companies. This is FALSE.

9 The following ideas support the concept of job enrichment:

a Herzberg's theory that job interest is a motivator.

d McGregor's Theory Y: that people prefer to control themselves than be controlled from above.

e Hackman and Oldham's theories about the prerequisites for internal motivation.

Self-assessment 4 1 a 'Get to know your team members well.' is GOOD advice, because no two people are the same – we all have our little quirks.

b 'Try to improve their working conditions.' is GOOD advice **only** if working conditions are so bad that morale has deteriorated.

c 'Give them more scope and more involvement' is GOOD advice because the opportunity to develop is often one of the major attractions of the job.

d 'Watch them more closely, so they know you care about them.' is generally bad advice; this is the opposite of increasing autonomy.

2   ALL these can be said to be dangers involved in delegation, to some extent:

a That jobs will be delegated for things which the team leader must retain personal responsibility for – such as safety. This **is** a danger, because there are some jobs which the team leader can't afford to delegate.

b That jobs will be delegated which everyone finds boring and unrewarding. This **is** a danger, because it won't enrich anyone's work.

c That team members will not carry out the jobs correctly. This **is** a danger, if the leader doesn't give proper instruction, or doesn't monitor performance.

d That a team member will find the new job so rewarding that he or she will lose interest in other work. – This **is** a danger, and one which, in a sense is a danger of all job enrichment. Obviously, if people are to develop, they will want to progress to more interesting work.

3   You may have included:

- controlling the pace of the work;
- determining the order or sequence in which the work is done;
- deciding how the work is done;
- deciding when the work is done;
- choosing the tools, equipment or materials used for the job;
- influencing the quality of work produced;
- deciding where the work is done.

5 Answers to activities

Activity 6 on page 13

	Physiological	Safety	Love	Esteem	Self-actualization
A drinking fountain	✓				
A feeling that you are attaining your career ambition.					✓
A comfortable working temperature.	✓	✓			
Meeting well the demands of your job.				✓	
Being accepted as a valued member of a working group.			✓		
Breathing equipment for a firefighter.		✓			
Enjoying the respect of your boss.				✓	

Activity 31 on page 54

A possible set of answers is given in the following table. You may have included some that are more relevant to your own organization.

Physiological

- Canteen facilities
- Sleeping bags and tents
- Survival packs
- Drinking fountains
- Rest rooms
- Coffee breaks

Safety

- Safe working conditions
- Protective clothing
- First aid kits
- Pension and sick pay schemes
- Agreements on work procedures

Love

- The chance to work in a group
- Social clubs, etc.
- The opportunity to help others
- Rest rooms and canteen facilities where people can meet

Esteem

- Praise for work done
- Status symbols
- Recognition as a valued employee
- Job title and its associated authority
- Self-respect from achieving success at work

Self-actualization

- Interesting work
- The chance to be creative
- Challenging work
- The chance to develop skills and talents

6 Answers to the quick quiz

Answer 1   You may have answered something like: 'What makes you really want to do something.' or 'What makes you want to work, instead of just doing it because you have to.'

Answer 2   The Maslow list of needs, from 'lowest' to 'highest' are: physiological, safety, love, esteem and self-actualization.

Answer 3   Theory X suggests the 'stick and carrot' approach – offering money and security, and threatening people.

Answer 4   Theory Y says that people do not dislike work and under the right conditions will enjoy it.

85

Answer 5   A maintenance factor is something which can cause dissatisfaction when it isn't present, but will not motivate by itself.

Answer 6   Performance depends on effort. Effort depends on motivation.

Answer 7   The reward may not be seen to be attractive enough, or attractive but unattainable.

Answer 8   Disadvantages are: high absenteeism and labour turnover, more accidents and higher costs.

Answer 9   They are feedback from the job, autonomy, skill variety, task identity and task significance.

Answer 10   Job enlargement means giving more tasks of similar complexity.

Answer 11   Job rotation is giving people a variety of jobs of the same complexity.

Answer 12   Jobs where job satisfaction is low; maintenance factors are costly; changes would not be expensive; lack of motivation is affecting performance.

Answer 13   (a) Feedback should be given promptly – as soon as possible after the results of the work are known. (b) The best kind of feedback is detailed information, given in a positive and tactful way.

Answer 14   Autonomy is 'self-government': the authority to do your job as you see fit.

Answer 15   You could have mentioned quite a number of things, including: following the principles of job enrichment; aiming to get the right kind of atmosphere; valuing effort and personal contribution; promoting the intrinsic worth of the job; making work fun.

7 Certificate

Completion of this certificate by an authorized person shows that you have worked through all the parts of this workbook and satisfactorily completed the assessments. The certificate provides a record of what you have done that may be used for exemptions or as evidence of prior learning against other nationally certificated qualifications.

Pergamon Open Learning and NEBS Management are always keen to refine and improve their products. One of the key sources of information to help this process are people who have just used the product. If you have any information or views, good or bad, please pass these on.

NEBS
MANAGEMENT
DEVELOPMENT

SUPER SERIES

THIRD EDITION

Motivating People

....

has satisfactorily completed this workbook

Name of signatory ....

Position ....

Signature ....

Date ....

Official stamp

SUPER SERIES

SUPER SERIES 3

0-7506-3362-X   Full Set of Workbooks, User Guide and Support Guide

A. Managing Activities

B. Managing Resources

C. Managing People

D. Managing Information

SUPER SERIES 3 USER GUIDE + SUPPORT GUIDE

SUPER SERIES 3 CASSETTE TITLES

To Order - phone us direct for prices and availability details
(please quote ISBNs when ordering)
College orders: 01865 314333 • Account holders: 01865 314301
Individual purchases: 01865 314627 (please have credit card details ready)

We Need Your Views

We really need your views in order to make the Super Series 3 (SS3) an even better learning tool for you. Please take time out to complete and return this questionnaire to Trudi Righton, Pergamon Open Learning, Linacre House, Jordan Hill, Oxford, OX2 8DP.

Name :..

Address :...

....

Title of workbook :..

If applicable, please state which qualification you are studying for. If not, please describe what study you are undertaking, and with which organisation or college:

....

Please grade the following out of 10 (10 being extremely good, 0 being extremely poor):

Content   ....   Appropriateness to your position   ....

Readability   ....   Qualification coverage   ....

What did you particularly like about this workbook?
....
....
....

Are there any features you disliked about this workbook? Please identify them.
....
....
....

Are there any errors we have missed? If so, please state page number: ....

How are you using the material? For example, as an open learning course, as a reference resource, as a training resource etc.
....

How did you hear about Super Series 3?:

Word of mouth: ☐   Through my tutor/trainer: ☐   Mailshot: ☐

Other (please give details):...
....

Many thanks for your help in returning this form.